When you think of Jewish food, a few classics come to mind: chicken soup with matzo balls, challah, maybe a babka if you're feeling adventurous. But as food writer and nice Jewish boy Jake Cohen demonstrates in this stunning debut cookbook, Jewish food can be so much more. In *Jew-ish*, he reinvents the food of his Ashkenazi heritage and draws inspiration from his husband's Persian-Iraqi traditions to offer recipes that are modern, fresh, and enticing for a whole new generation of readers. Imagine the components of an everything bagel wrapped into a flaky galette, latkes dyed vibrant yellow with saffron for a Persian spin on the potato pancake, plus best-ever hybrid desserts like Macaroon Brownies and Pumpkin Spice Babka! From elevated yet approachable classics like Jake's Perfect Challah, Roasted Tomato Brisket, Short Rib Cholent, and Iraqi Beet Kubbeh Soup to innovative creations like Cacio e Pepe Rugelach, Sabich Bagel Sandwiches, and Matzo Tiramisu, *Jew-ish* is a brilliant collection of delicious recipes—but it's also much more than that. As Jake reconciles ancient traditions with our modern times, his recipes become a celebration of a rich and vibrant history, a love story of blending cultures, and an invitation to gather around the table and create new memories with family, friends, and loved ones.

jew-ish

A COOKBOOK

jew-ish

REINVENTED RECIPES
FROM A MODERN MENSCH

A COOKBOOK BY JAKE COHEN

PHOTOGRAPHY BY MATT TAYLOR-GROSS

HOUGHTON MIFFLIN HARCOURT BOSTON NEW YORK

Photography copyright © 2021 by Matt Taylor-Gross
Food styling by Barrett Washburne
Prop styling by Marie Sullivan

hmhbooks.com

Library of Congress Cataloging-in-Publication Data
Names: Cohen, Jake, 1993– author.
Title: Jew-ish : reinvented recipes from a modern
    mensch : a cookbook / by Jake Cohen ;
    photography by Matt Taylor-Gross.
Description: Boston : Houghton Mifflin Harcourt, 2021. |
    Includes index.
Identifiers: LCCN 2020036239 (print) | LCCN
    2020036240 (ebook) | ISBN 9780358353980
    (hardback) | ISBN 9780358354253 (ebook)
Subjects: LCSH: Jewish cooking. | LCGFT: Cookbooks.
Classification: LCC TX724 .C538 2021 (print) |
    LCC TX724 (ebook) | DDC 641.5/676—dc23
LC record available at https://lccn.loc.
    gov/2020036239
LC ebook record available at https://lccn.loc.
    gov/2020036240

Book design by Mia Johnson

Printed in the United States of America

DOC 10 9 8 7 6 5 4 3

PO 4500821403

3 2021

For Alex:
this book is
nothing short
of our
love story

CONTENTS

Introduction viii

High Holidays of Our Lives

excuse me,
are you jew-ish?

Secular Jews in America (my family included) have self-identified as Jew-*ish* long before using -*ish* in the title of just about anything became all the rage. Just a pause and a little extra stress on the *"-ish"* are enough to tell the world that while you may be Jewish by blood, you're not necessarily going to shul on Saturday, turning off your phone on the Sabbath, or saying no to a bacon cheeseburger.

Growing up, I didn't really have a strong connection with my Jewish identity. I was Jew-*ish*, and aside from the obligatory bar mitzvah, that was about it. In fact, after coming out at eighteen, I felt more connected to my queerness than I ever had to my Jewishness. As far as coming out stories go, I was one of the lucky ones—I was fully embraced by my family and friends. Even though I had it easy, I quickly felt that living an openly, unapologetically queer life came with a certain responsibility—a sense of obligation to show queers living in not-so-accepting, or even dangerous, parts of the world that a normal life was not only possible, but something to fight for. Pride is something that has been ingrained in me, at least as it pertains to my sexuality.

I had never quite felt the same sense of pride in being Jewish, but I had never felt shame about it, either—I felt as I think most young Jews in America do: indifferent. Most secular Jews living in America today have been lucky enough to be sheltered from hate. That's not to say we aren't aware of the atrocities that have happened to our community and how close to home they hit. And it's not like antisemitism isn't still horrifyingly ubiquitous, and growing, today—it certainly is. But the day-to-day experiences of white, non-practicing Jewish people in today's America are likely far removed from those of minority groups whose differences are more visible. This is probably why, when I was growing up, being Jewish didn't really feel like a big deal to me.

At the time I met my husband, Alex, we both identified as Jew-*ish*, but to varying degrees. I was what you would call a High Holiday Jew, the kind who comes out of the secular woodwork around Passover, Rosh Hashanah, and Yom Kippur to completely commit to temple, gefilte fish, and Manischewitz. Alex was what you would call a no-holiday Jew. He had grown up with a healthy dose of Jewish familial meshugas, but rarely celebrated High Holidays and didn't even get bar-mitzvahed. These were our individual narratives when we started dating, but together we decided that it was important to us to define what our Jew-*ish* practice would look like as a couple.

At one point, we even thought about joining a synagogue. We had already gone to a few High Holiday services together, and on each occasion, we had been moved by the sense of togetherness and the poetic, insightful sermons that ignited deep reflection. We thought that maybe by going

to Friday-night services more regularly, we'd not only become more connected to our Jewishness, but also build a community and a more thoughtful perspective on life. After giving services a try at a few different temples, though, we determined that synagogue wasn't for us. That's when we started hosting Shabbat.

Shabbat became exactly the kind of space Alex and I were looking for to define our Jewish practice. Shabbat was about all the things we had been hoping to gain from synagogue, without the dogmatic subtext. It wasn't about spirituality, religion, or reciting Hebrew prayers. It was about taking a moment at the end of the week to pause and actively exercise gratitude, to strengthen and build our community, and to simultaneously do the one thing we enjoy most—eat.

Through hosting Shabbat, I found myself fostering a new appreciation for Jewish cuisine, and I began to adapt recipes from all across the Diaspora. I dedicated time to learning and perfecting the Ashkenazi dishes of my childhood, becoming increasingly confident in my brisket, matzo balls, and kugel. Alex is a Mizrahi Jew, and through his maternal family, I have been exposed to and able to absorb a mix of Persian Jewish and Iraqi Jewish culinary traditions, which are rich in fragrant rices, hearty stews, and cardamom-kissed desserts. Similar to those of Eastern Europe, many of these recipes have traveled long and far, surviving wars and persecution, to reach the surface of my Shabbos table. Beyond tackling and blending the dishes familiar to Alex and myself, I've even adapted a number of Sephardic and Yemeni recipes foreign to us both, expanding our understanding of and appreciation for the diverse Jewish culinary traditions across the world.

Jewish food is constantly evolving. It's a cuisine largely composed of old-country dishes that have traveled with the Diaspora, marrying with the flavors of new places the Jews have settled, often as a result of fleeing persecution. New countries always came with new local culinary customs and the availability of new ingredients. The only constant was a desire to hold on to the food of our people, in whatever regional variation that became—whether jalapeño-laced matzo ball soup in Mexico or maple-scented challah in Canada. All such dishes are still inherently Jewish and join the ever-expanding culinary lexicon of the Tribe.

This book is a compilation of recipes I have developed along this journey of hosting Shabbat, a journey wherein Alex and I have had the chance to explore our Jewish identities together. Some are traditional, many aren't, and all are close to my heart—either by evoking my Ashkenazi upbringing, symbolizing my absorption of Mizrahi traditions through marriage, representing my discovery of new and equally meaningful Jewish stories through food, or some combination of the three. Don't get me wrong—I get very heated about steering away from my family's tradition when it comes to many Jewish foods (just wait until you read my thoughts on brisket!), but at the end of the day, we must celebrate any form of Jewish culture, old or new.

For some reason, I have teared up every time I've tried to write this introduction. I mean, I'm not overly sentimental, and it's not like babka is going to bring peace to the Middle East. Yet somehow, no matter where I am, the waterworks begin when I start writing about my connection to Judaism. I'm not necessarily observant or kosher or even able to articulate my belief in a higher power or lack thereof. I just think it's because this is the final section of the book I wrote, encapsulating not only these recipes and stories tied to those I care for the most, but my journey to a greater understanding of my identity.

This book has helped me define the pride I have for the rich culture of traditions and dishes I've inherited. It's a love story. It's a family tree. It's me at my core. It's Jew-*ish*.

friday-night bites

Let's talk about Shabbat. Just to be clear, I'm not talking about schlepping to temple or doing anything spiritual. I'm talking about reserving Friday evening at the end of a crazy workweek to pause, reflect, and recharge while breaking bread with loved ones. Shabbat is the OG dinner party. It's self-care through a lush spread of food and wine; no wonder it's never gone out of style.

Before we get into the nitty gritty, let's set aside any expectations around what you "should" or "shouldn't" be doing on the Sabbath. I have a pretty progressive mentality toward Shabbat—which probably stems from the fact that I was brought up not observing it. Old schoolers would say Shabbat *must* commence at sundown, and once the Sabbath begins, you can't even flip a light switch. I always invite my guests to arrive for Shabbat dinner at seven p.m., because I care more about my husband making it on time from work than I do about the relative position of celestial bodies. Post-sundown, not only do I toggle the lights, I also don't turn off my phone. (Have you seen a social media addict in withdrawal? It's ugly.) Long story short, Shabbat is a tradition that you can make your own, in whatever way works for you. The only real rule is that it has to be on Friday. At night. Otherwise, it's pretty much just a meal with friends.

Shabbat has become the most important Jewish ritual in my life (though sending food back at restaurants and complaining constantly about how hot or cold it is are close runners-up). My love for this age-old tradition was ignited a few years ago upon discovering OneTable, a nonprofit organization, of which I'm now a proud board member. OneTable's mission is to empower individuals in their twenties and thirties to build an authentic, sustainable, and valuable Shabbat practice. With the help of OneTable, I felt I had the permission and guidance to build a practice that fit my life and my priorities. I found an unmatched joy in hosting others, and when you invite someone over for dinner—especially someone you've never met before—you not only build a bridge that connects you with that individual, but you also engage in a ritual quite similar to that of giving a gift. As a host, you should delight in the act of inviting your guests (and if not, consider revising your list!). Likewise, your guests should delight in receiving and accepting your invitation. There is a magic to this reciprocity that imparts a layer of warmth to both new and long-standing relationships. It's no wonder that after just a few Shabbats, I was able to both deepen existing friendships and quickly build many new ones. I discovered the rich community that I craved but previously didn't know how to build.

what to expect when you're expecting . . . guests

Whether you're starting a new Shabbat practice, igniting an old one, or just looking for general dinner party tips, I'm here to help you build a healthy relationship with hospitality. The following are the three key things to keep in mind when hosting.

Work with the space you've got. Try not to let the circumstances around your space or your possessions prevent you from hosting. First off, you don't need napkin rings, fancy plates, or crystal glasses to break bread. Don't have a big table? No problem—let your guests sit wherever there's room, even if that's on the couch, bed, or floor. Alex and I lived in a studio during our first few years together. When we hosted, our friends would take over the couch and coffee table, while we sat on the edge of the bed with dinner trays. Plastic plates, paper napkins, no frills. Don't let yourself get bogged down by a particular set of expectations. Entertaining is about sharing a meal and an experience. It's about having a good time in good company—not re-creating a dinner scene from a Nancy Meyers movie.

You don't have to do it alone. I'm a glutton for punishment. I take on too much and have true difficulty saying no to people, especially when it comes to entertaining. "Can I bring a friend to your Shabbat?" Sure! "Can you make an extra dessert for Passover?" Of course! "Will you cater my nephew's bris?" . . . Okay, I'd probably say no to that one. The point is, sometimes as a host, you may feel like you've taken on too much. But remember: not everything has to be on you. Delegate tasks to your guests. Things like bringing wine or challah are unimposing requests that can be divided among invitees but will add up to a meaningful reduction in your workload. If the prep work has you stressed out, ask a supportive spouse, friend, or family member to lend a hand. My husband has learned to style cheese boards like a pro and sets gorgeous tables with intricate Pinterest-inspired napkin folds. My mother has made countless supermarket runs on my behalf, giving me the extra time I need to cook. Hosting is hard work, so don't be afraid to lean on others for help.

There's no place like mise en place. This French term, meaning "put in place," was ingrained in me throughout culinary school and during my time working in restaurants. It refers to having all the ingredients, tools, and equipment you need to properly execute a meal prepared and organized (i.e., chopped up, measured out, set aside in bowls, etc.) to set you up for success. Extending this principle more generally, if there is anything you can prepare and organize in advance, do it. When I'm getting ready for Shabbat, whatever I can make early and reheat day-of is done the night before. I set table the morning of, before I go to work, with all the serving platters set out and ready to go. I have the cheese board laid out half an hour before my guests arrive, and I open a bottle each of red wine and white wine (chilled the night before) several minutes before the first guest rings the doorbell. Proper mise en place is not only a technique to help you host with ease, but also a mindset that will give you the confidence that you've got this dinner under control. Because you do.

just like a prayer, i'll take you there

In my Friday-night practice, I like to incorporate three classic rituals: candles, wine, and bread. On the surface, because these items are present in almost any formal dinner situation, they seem borderline banal (and they'll certainly be inoffensive to any of your Shabbat guests, Jewish and non-Jewish alike). What restaurant these days doesn't serve dinner accompanied by tealights, sourdough, and Pinot Noir by the glass? In the context of a Shabbat practice, however, these elements take on new meanings, and perhaps give us space to reflect on how the simplest things can be deeply profound—and sometimes, even magical. On the following pages, I give some suggestions as to what meaning the candles, wine, and bread might take on, along with some prayers that are traditionally recited to sanctify these elements. Ultimately, though, your Shabbat practice is yours to make your own. Want to add or subtract some new symbols, or have none at all? Go for it! Want to say the prayers in English since you don't understand Hebrew? Bless! Want to ditch the prayers altogether? Great, let's keep it nondenominational! I've thrown in some alternative readings curated by OneTable's Rabbi Jessica Minnen. It's your Shabbat dinner, so you get to take control and you get to define the vibe.

get lit.

Shabbat signifies the end of the workweek, where lighting the candles is the final act. Or, more simply put, fire = weekend. The common practice is to light two candles. Why do we light two? Well, as is the case with many Jewish traditions, we don't really know, since it's not in the Torah. But the rabbinic scholars link it to the two commandments to keep and remember Shabbat. My favorite quote from Rabbi Minnen is, "The beauty of Jewish tradition is not its certitude but its ambiguity; even the rabbis disagree on what it means to keep and remember Shabbat." Some people light two candles for the household. Some even light two per person. I typically have two candlesticks and I try to have a tealight for every guest, so that everyone can get in on the action.

The Hebrew Prayer

בָּרוּךְ אַתָּה אַדְנָי אֱלֹהֵינוּ מֶלֶךְ הָעוֹלָם אֲשֶׁר קִדְשָׁנוּ בְּמִצְוֹתָיו וְצִוָּנוּ לְהַדְלִיק נֵר שֶׁל שַׁבָּת

Baruch atah, Adonai Eloheinu, Melech haolam, asher kid'shanu b'mitzvotav, v'tzivanu l'hadlik ner shel Shabbat.

THE MEANING

Blessed are you, Infinite One, Who makes us holy through our actions and honors us with light of Shabbat.

AN ALTERNATIVE READING

"On Shabbat, the light within everyone and everything is revealed. We need only the will to see it."
—*Sefat Emet (1847–1905, Poland)*

The Exercise

Go around the table and have each person say one thing that lit up their week and for which they'd like to express some gratitude. If it's a really big party, make your guests introduce themselves to someone they don't know to share their highlights.

turn up.

Wine is important in any meal, but crucial on Shabbat. It's what we use to sanctify the Sabbath. It enhances the moment and makes it special. Its presence distinguishes Shabbat even further from the mundane and from the workweek. For some people, wine even imparts a level of holiness. For others, it's there for you to get tipsy. Once again—you do you.

The Hebrew Prayer

בָּרוּךְ אַתָּה אַדֹנָי אֱלֹהֵינוּ מֶלֶךְ הָעוֹלָם בּוֹרֵא פְּרִי הַגָּפֶן

Baruch ata Adonai, Eloheinu Melech ha-olam, boreh p'ri hagafen.

THE MEANING

Blessed are you, Infinite One, Creator of the vine.

AN ALTERNATIVE READING

"During the week . . . we lose some of the light in our eyes; it is restored to us by the reflection of light in our kiddush cup."
—*Talmud Bavli, Shabbat 113b*

The Exercise

Make a toast to someone at the table. Yes, the host should get plenty of love, but make sure you shine light on all the *shayna punims* gathered around the table.

challah back.

Nothing melts away the craziness of a week like tearing into a warm, freshly baked challah. We don't *technically* need to dive into why it's the best bread, but we will. It's fluffy and tender, with the perfect balance of sweetness and salinity. It's also highly versatile: not only is it the star of the Shabbos table, but it frequently makes cameos as French toast, sandwich bread, and even the occasional hot dog bun. It's simply a superior loaf!

But beyond the enjoyment we get from eating it lies the true beauty in what it represents on the table. It symbolizes nourishment and allows us to reflect on our gratitude for being nourished. Also, it is customary to serve two loaves to symbolize abundance. Finally, challah is meant to be ripped with one's hands and passed around. This experience of physically breaking bread with others connects everyone around the table, turning strangers into friends and friends into family.

The Hebrew Prayer

בָּרוּךְ אַתָּה אַדֹנָי אֱלֹהֵינוּ מֶלֶךְ הָעוֹלָם הַמּוֹצִיא לֶחֶם מִן הָאָרֶץ

Baruch ata Adonai, Eloheinu Melech ha-olam, hamotzi lechem min ha'aretz.

THE MEANING

Blessed are you, Infinite One, Who brings forth bread from the Earth.

AN ALTERNATIVE READING

"On Shabbat, challah represents a taste of *tikkun olam,* the possibility of the world restored."
—*The Maharal of Prague*

The Exercise

Former OneTable staffer Zoe Plotsky brought this tradition to my Shabbat table straight from her days at Jewish sleepaway camp. Have everyone present touch the challah at the same time (if there are a lot of people, touch somebody who's touching the challah). Then, all together, say the prayer for the bread, or any other dedication of your preference. Afterward, tear off a piece of challah and pass the loaf around.

The Recipe →

Jake's Perfect Challah

YIELD: MAKES 1 LARGE LOAF

PREP TIME: 40 MINUTES, PLUS 2 HOURS 30 MINUTES PROOFING TIME

COOK TIME: 35 MINUTES

1 cup water, heated to 115°F

½ cup (100g) granulated sugar

1 (¼-ounce) packet active dry yeast (2¼ teaspoons)

6 tablespoons vegetable oil

¼ cup honey

4 large eggs

5½ to 6 cups (745g to 810g) all-purpose flour, plus more for dusting

2 teaspoons kosher salt

1½ teaspoons assorted seeds, such as sesame, fennel, poppy, nigella, and/ or cumin, for garnish

Flaky sea salt, for garnish

1 In the bowl of a stand mixer fitted with the whisk attachment, mix the warm water and 2 tablespoons of the sugar to dissolve, then sprinkle the yeast over the top. Let stand until foamy, 5 to 10 minutes. Add the remaining 6 tablespoons sugar, 4 tablespoons of the vegetable oil, honey, and 3 of the eggs, then whisk on medium speed until incorporated.

2 Switch to the dough hook. Add 5½ cups flour and the salt to the mixture in the bowl and, beginning on low speed and gradually increasing to medium, knead until a smooth, elastic dough forms, 3 to 4 minutes. (Your dough will be tacky but shouldn't be sticky. If it's sticky, mix in additional flour, a few tablespoons at a time, until tacky.) Transfer to a lightly floured work surface with floured hands and continue to knead by hand, dusting with flour as needed, until a very smooth ball forms, another 3 to 5 minutes. (Alternatively, if you make this dough entirely by hand, it will require about 10 minutes of kneading on a clean work surface after incorporating the flour.) Grease a medium bowl and your hands with the remaining 2 tablespoons of vegetable oil and add the dough ball, turning gently to coat. Cover with plastic wrap or a kitchen towel and set aside in a warm place until doubled in size, 1½ to 2 hours.

3 Transfer the dough to a clean work surface and divide into 6 equal pieces. Roll each into a long rope, about 18 inches in length and slightly thicker at the center and thinner at both ends. Lay out all the ropes vertically, then link the top of each rope and pinch together to seal, tucking the sealed end under itself slightly.

4 Take the outer two ropes and cross them over each other to switch places, crossing the rope from the right under the rope from the left. Take the farthest rope on the right and cross it over to be in the middle (with 3 ropes on the left of it and 2 ropes on the right). Then, take the second rope from the left and cross it all the way to the far right. Now, take the farthest rope to the left and move it to the middle (with 2 ropes on the left of it and 3 ropes on the right). Take the second rope from the right and cross it all the way to the far left. Repeat this process until there are no more ropes to braid, then pinch the ends and tuck them under the end of the challah. (See pictures and instructions on the next page.) Using your hands, carefully transfer the challah to a parchment-lined half sheet pan, placing it on a diagonal.

5 Beat the remaining egg and brush liberally on the challah. Let the challah rise again, uncovered, until doubled in volume, about 1 hour.

6 Preheat the oven to 350°F.

7 Brush the challah again with the remaining beaten egg, then sprinkle with the seeds and a heavy pinch of flaky salt.

8 Bake, rotating the pan halfway through the cooking time, for 35 to 40 minutes, until the challah is golden brown and has reached an internal temperature of 190°F. Remove from the oven and let cool completely before slicing. Serve the challah the same day you bake it.

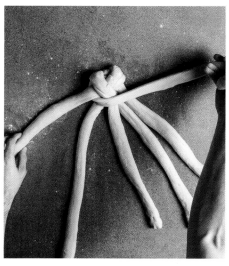

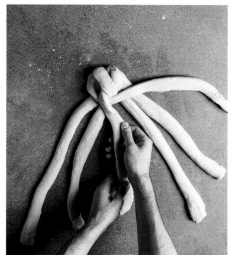

1 Lay out all the ropes vertically, then link the top of each rope and pinch together to seal, tucking the sealed end under itself slightly.

2 Take the outer two ropes and cross them over each other to switch places, crossing the rope from the right under the rope from the left.

3 Take the farthest rope on the right and cross it over to be in the middle (with 3 ropes on the left of it and 2 ropes on the right).

4 Take the second rope from the left and cross it all the way to the far right.

5 Take the farthest rope to the left and move it to the middle.

6 Take the second rope from the right and cross it all the way to the far left.

7 Return to step 3 and repeat until all the dough is braided, then pinch the ends to seal and tuck the sealed end under.

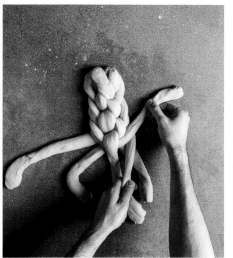

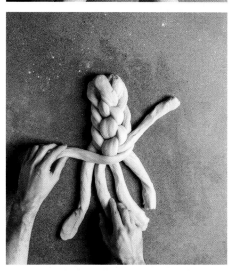

! I love serving up one ornate
• challah at Shabbat, but if you're keen on serving two for tradition, you can easily split this dough in half before dividing it into balls, rolling, and braiding. They can be baked on the same half sheet pan—just be sure to space them at least 4 inches apart.

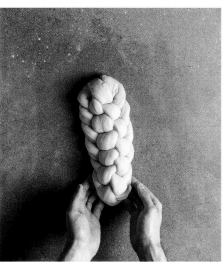

my pantry

things i buy

MATZO MEAL

I have a can of Manischewitz matzo meal on hand at all times. Past matzo balls, it's my favorite binder for my perfect latkes (see page 77). The fact is, it's just matzo crushed into crumbs, so if you've got matzo and a food processor, matzo meal is just a few pulses away.

EGG NOODLES

Absorbed into the Jewish food scene from the Ashkenazi kitchen in Eastern Europe, egg noodles are a sure sign that comfort food is on its way. Whether for a cozy kugel or a reviving bowl of chicken noodle soup, I only use wide egg noodles, and I won't ever be convinced to use any other size nood.

SOUR CREAM AND CREAM CHEESE

These are just as important to Ashkenazi cooking as butter is to French cuisine. Always go for full-fat—you're worth it, and it makes a world of difference in cheesecake and kugel.

PICKLES

I had every intention of giving you a half-sour pickle recipe in this book, but after many tests, I just was never as happy with my cuke skills as I was with the pickle spears sold in giant buckets by the guys at the farmers' market. I came to the realization that making homemade pickles is a passion project for bearded Brooklyn hipsters—the average person doesn't have time for lacto-fermentation, and neither do I. That being said, my fridge is always stocked with both kosher dill and half-sour pickles for snacking, and you better save the brine! It's great for braising cabbage (see page 115) and the occasional pickleback shot.

DATE SYRUP

Also known as *silan*, this thick, amber syrup made from cooked-down dates is easily my favorite natural sweetener. Whether drizzled over yogurt in the morning or tossed with vegetables before roasting to encourage a little extra caramelization, date syrup adds a fruity sweetness that doesn't overpower like maple syrup can. Soom and Just Date Syrup are my two favorite brands, especially since they come in squeeze bottles to prevent a sticky situation.

POMEGRANATE MOLASSES

This is what you get when you cook down pomegranate juice until it's as thick as molasses. The tartness from the fruit makes for a sweetener that adds bright acidity to any dip or marinade. I love whisking it into salad dressings, drizzling it over meats as a glaze, and incorporating it into BBQ sauce (see page 61) to add an unexpected tang.

BASMATI RICE

I was blind to the nuances of rice until I met my husband. His mother and aunts always stressed the importance of high-quality long-grain rice for cooking any Persian rice dish, and they're so right. Using this sort of rice ensures the grains don't stick together and stay fluffy even when encased in a crispy, crunchy *tahdig*. Given the impossibility of importing Iranian rice, Indian basmati is the best option to always have in your pantry.

ROSE WATER

I love foods that taste like perfume. There is nothing more enticing to me than the floral punch rose water adds to desserts and cocktails (it's a great addition to any batch of simple syrup), but in moderation. Get a bottle and it will last you forever, given that any recipe will only need a splash of rose water to give you all the flower power you want.

TAHINI

You know it. You love it. This Middle Eastern sesame paste is a staple in my pantry for pureeing into hummus, drizzling over honestly anything, and adding peanut butter–like richness to any dessert. Oh, and it's used to make halva, which is one of my top-five favorite sweets! The thing about tahini is, quality really matters. A good tahini will be smooth, rich, and nutty in flavor, without the bitterness you can often taste in inferior brands. My kitchen always has a jar of Seed + Mill tahini (I'm obsessed with their halva, too) and another of Soom brand on hand. Just be sure to give it an enthusiastic stir before drizzling.

SAFFRON

Truly the most luxe thing in my pantry, these crimson strands are the stigmas of crocus flowers that are hand-plucked and dried in an extremely labor-intensive process that makes saffron more expensive by weight than gold. That being said, you won't break the bank since you only need a small pinch at a time to grind and brew into saffron water for anything from crispy Persian rice

to syrup-soaked desserts. I get a constant stream of top-shelf Iranian saffron from my husband's family—though I have no clue how it's being smuggled in—which has taught me what to look for when buying it. You want long, thick, bright red strands that aren't shriveled. Once you've got it home, you should always store your saffron in a cool, dry, dark place. My mother-in-law keeps hers in the freezer, which also makes it much easier to grind into a powder.

CRUSHED ALEPPO PEPPER

I use this almost as much as I use freshly cracked black pepper. These crushed Syrian chiles are not only vibrant red in color, they're slightly milder and finer than regular crushed red pepper, so you can use a healthy sprinkle to finish any dish for a true pop in both appearance and taste.

URFA BIBER

While most chiles can add heat, these sun-dried Turkish peppers add a deep smokiness that I'm obsessed with. Whenever I'm frying garlic for any application, I find throwing in a pinch of these oily flakes adds a depth of flavor and spice that most other crushed chiles can't. Unless you have a great spice store nearby, your best bet is ordering it online; I love the Urfa biber from Burlap & Barrel.

HARISSA

This oily, North African red chile paste is like supercharged hot sauce. In addition to roasted red peppers and chiles, it's perfumed with spices like cumin and coriander for a condiment that adds as much heat as it does flavor. A kitchen staple of Moroccan and Tunisian Jews, harissa is great in marinades, stir-fries, and especially tomato sauce. I love harissa from New York Shuk, a local Brooklyn brand that even offers a variety flavored with preserved lemon for another layer of complexity.

AMBA

If you love Jewish Diaspora history, you'll love *amba!* The Jews of Iraq were instrumental in the spice trade with India, finding culinary inspiration along the way, as with *amba,* which blends pickled mango with spices and chiles into a spicy and lip-smacking sauce. When the Jews were expelled from Iraq in 1950, they brought the condiment to Israel, where you'll see it as part of *sabich,* an Israeli pita packed with the traditional Iraqi Shabbat breakfast of fried eggplant and hard-boiled eggs. While you can use it as a catchall condiment, there's nothing quite like the combo of *amba* and eggs. I find myself reaching for the jar most days I make breakfast. If you're ready to step up your morning yolk porn, you can find it easily online or at many specialty spice shops.

BAHARAT

My buddy and chef extraordinaire Zach Engel once told me that *baharat* is Middle Eastern pumpkin spice, and I've never been able to think of it any other way. A staple in Iraqi Jewish cooking, this Arabic spice blend can contain everything from cardamom and cinnamon to cloves, black pepper, nutmeg, cumin, fennel, coriander, rose petals, and more, depending on who's grinding it. Most famously used to season *t'beet,* a classic Iraqi baked chicken and rice dish, *baharat* is great whenever a dish, from meats to desserts, needs an earthy warmth. La Boîte makes a great blend, if you're looking to cozy up to pumpkin spice's sexier cousin.

SUMAC

You need sumac in your life. This spice, made from ground dried sumac berries, adds a bright acidity to anything it touches, like a spritz of fresh lemon. Traditionally sprinkled over Middle Eastern dips and salads, I've never found a dish it wouldn't improve (it's especially great when paired with chocolate). You can typically find it in the spice section of most supermarkets, but my favorite variety is the cured Turkish sumac from Burlap & Barrel. I even pack a jar of it in my carry-on when I travel.

DRIED FENUGREEK LEAVES

I first bought dried fenugreek leaves to make *ghormeh sabzi* (see page 149), a hearty Persian stew of meat, greens, and beans. When I opened the bag, I was punched in the face with the sugary aroma of maple, though the flavor is delicate, somewhere between celery and fennel. A pinch goes a long way, but it's one of my favorite secrets for adding a bit of brightness to any dish. You can typically find these dried leaves, as well as fenugreek seeds and fresh or frozen leaves (sometimes labeled *methi*), at Indian and Middle Eastern spice stores (and always online).

TURMERIC

It's earthy, it's supposedly good for you, and it will stain anything it touches. I adore ground turmeric and the subtle mustard flavor and golden color it adds to any dish. A common ingredient in Middle Eastern cooking, it really sings when married with other spices like cumin and cayenne. Wasn't kidding about the staining, though. I'm definitely not wearing white if this jar is out of the spice cabinet.

ZA'ATAR

The ingredients in this Arabic spice blend can vary greatly depending on where you land in the Middle East. Typically, it's some combination of dried oregano, thyme, marjoram, and bible hyssop (which is also called za'atar and is what the blend is named after) blended with sumac and toasted sesame seeds. The resulting mixture is earthy and floral and tangy and nutty and absolutely stunning in any application. You can sprinkle it on chicken before roasting instead of the classic mixture of woody herbs. You can whisk it into salad dressings for complexity when paired with crunchy cucumbers, juicy tomatoes, and briny feta. You can bloom it in hot oil to drizzle over everything from pita to popcorn. Get creative with this essential flavor of the Levant. My favorite blends are from Burlap & Barrel and New York Shuk.

PRESERVED LEMONS

This ingredient is what happens when lemons are flavored with lemons. Submerged in a brine of lemon juice and salt, preserved lemons take on a bright citrus flavor that's mild on tartness but intense on lemon flavor. While they're not difficult to make, they do take a few weeks to preserve, so I'm a big fan of buying them. Most supermarkets carry jarred preserved lemons, which may come as either small whole lemons or lemon halves. New York Shuk makes a preserved lemon paste that I love to spoon into dishes to add a little pucker.

DRIED BLACK PERSIAN LIMES

File this ingredient under things that look weird but taste amazing. A crucial flavoring to many Persian stews, these dried limes, or *limu Omani,* are little Ping-Pong balls of salt-brine-boiled and sun-dried citrus that add a bright, concentrated lime flavor with undertones of fermented tang. You can buy them whole (best for stews) or powdered (great for spice rubs for roasts), though always strive to get black limes, which are dried further and have more flavor than the brown variety. When cooking with them, always remember you can control the intensity of this powerful flavoring. After simmering for 15 minutes, pierce a few of the slightly softened limes with a paring knife, letting the tang diffuse throughout the stew. The more you pierce, the stronger the flavor. Just remember that dried limes add flavor, but are not for eating, so try to avoid serving them to your guests.

FLOUR

Of course, you have flour in your pantry. But do you *actually know* how to measure it? I stand by the golden rule that a measuring cup should never be shoved into a bag of flour, which compacts more flour into the cup than you think you're measuring. Instead, spoon flour into the measuring cup and level the top with a knife. Using a scale? In my kitchen, 1 cup all-purpose flour weighs 135g (or 4¾ ounces). I personally use King Arthur, not that you were asking.

SALT

What can be more Jewish than the fact that every food magazine and cookbook calls for kosher salt? No, that doesn't mean it's been blessed by your rabbi or mined by chosen people. Kosher salt is called that because it has a larger crystal size, making it perfect for drawing out the blood from meat during the koshering process. It also happens to be the ideal size for seasoning food and picking up pinches with your fingers. I'm a Diamond Crystal boy, the standard choice for every test kitchen I've ever worked in. If you use another brand, the dish may be more or less salty depending on the size of the salt crystals. For example, Morton kosher salt is finer than Diamond Crystal and therefore a teaspoon of Morton weighs more, making it "saltier." As for amounts, if I don't specify a measurement, then it's totally up to your taste. I'm heavy-handed with salt, while my mother hasn't touched the shaker since 2001.

things i make

SCHMALTZ

Butter is great, don't get me wrong. But few fats add as much flavor and richness as schmaltz—an essential ingredient to Ashkenazi cooking made from rendered chicken or goose fat, tradition-ally flavored with fried onions. You can get your hands on it one of two ways. You can head to the butcher or supermarket meat counter and buy containers of it. Or, if you cook as much chicken as I do, you can make it yourself! Save all the skin and fat trimmings you get before cook-ing, as well as those sweet pan drippings after roasting—not mandatory or traditional, but a personal favorite—and store them in the freezer. Once you have about 3 cups (¾ pound) skin and fat trimmings, combine them in a medium saucepan with whatever pan drippings you saved and enough water to just cover. Bring to a sim-mer and then cook over medium-low heat until all the water has evaporated and the chicken skin begins to brown, about 45 minutes. Throw in 1 yellow onion, minced, and cook until lightly caramelized, 8 to 10 minutes more. Strain through a fine-mesh sieve and let cool. (The strained fried chicken cracklings and onions are called *gribenes*, a shtetl classic, and should 100 percent be eaten fresh over bread or absolutely anything, with zero shame and zero expectation of sharing with others.) Store the schmaltz in an airtight container in the refrigerator for up to 1 month or in the freezer for up to 1 year.

COMPOUND SCHMALTZ

Now that you know I love schmaltz, you can understand why I'd zhuzh it up with garlic and herbs and lemon zest. Use it for any ap-plication in which you'd be using a compound butter! It's so luxe, you may even want to use it as conditioner. (Goodbye, split ends!) Just kidding about the hair care. Sort of. I always keep a batch in the freezer for weeknight roast chicken extravaganzas, so get ready for all this schmaltzy witchcraft!

YIELD: MAKES ABOUT 1 CUP
PREP TIME: 10 MINUTES

1 cup schmaltz (left), at room temperature

1 tablespoon minced fresh sage

1 tablespoon minced fresh rosemary

1 tablespoon minced fresh thyme

2 teaspoons kosher salt

1 teaspoon finely grated lemon zest

3 garlic cloves, finely grated

In a small bowl, stir together the schmaltz, sage, rosemary, thyme, salt, lemon zest, and garlic until well incorporated. Use immediately, or transfer to an airtight container and store in the refrigerator for up to 1 week or in the freezer for up to 6 months.

ONION CONFIT (AND VEGAN SCHMALTZ!)

Now that you understand that the flavor of cara-melized onions is one of the homiest and crucial flavors permeating Ashkenazi Jewish cooking, you can see why I would confit even more onions in schmaltz to make a super-savory, jammy onion relish. A spoonful of this adds that sweet slow-cooked allium flavor to even the simplest pasta or salad, and a bowl of the stuff is a stunner on any cheese board, giving fig jam a run for its money. Equally important, if you happen to be a vegetarian or vegan, use olive oil to confit the onions, and the resulting strained fat will be the closest schmaltz substitute you'll find. If you're not vegan, go for the schmaltz to add a double punch of caramelized onion flavor to your strained chicken fat.

YIELD: MAKES ABOUT 1 CUP
PREP TIME: 10 MINUTES, PLUS COOLING TIME
COOK TIME: 45 MINUTES

¾ cup schmaltz (opposite) or extra-virgin olive oil
2 medium yellow onions, minced
Kosher salt and freshly ground black pepper

In a small saucepan, combine the schmaltz, on-ions, and a heavy pinch each of salt and pepper over medium heat. Once bubbling, reduce the heat to maintain a low simmer and cook, stirring occasionally, until the onions are softened and beginning to caramelize, about 45 minutes. Let cool completely, then drain in a fine-mesh sieve set over a bowl. Transfer the onion confit to a jar and cover with a thin layer of the strained fat, then seal the jar and store in the refrigerator for up to 2 weeks. Store the remaining strained fat in an airtight container in the refrigerator for up to 1 week or in the freezer for up to 6 months.

SPICED BOURBON APPLESAUCE

Applesauce seems like such a daunting thing to make from scratch, but it honestly couldn't be easier. I take tart Granny Smiths and sim-mer them with oaky bourbon, brown sugar, and spices for a not-too-sweet applesauce with warm, boozy notes of caramel. Keep a jar in the fridge ready for breakfast, snacking, or dunking latkes (page 77).

YIELD: MAKES ABOUT 1 QUART
PREP TIME: 10 MINUTES, PLUS COOLING TIME
COOK TIME: 15 MINUTES

3 pounds Granny Smith apples (about 9 medium), peeled, cored, and coarsely chopped
1 cup bourbon whiskey
½ cup packed light brown sugar
1 teaspoon kosher salt
1 teaspoon ground cinnamon
¼ teaspoon freshly ground nutmeg
Grated zest and juice of 1 lemon

In a medium saucepan, combine the apples, whiskey, brown sugar, salt, cinnamon, nutmeg, and lemon zest and juice. Bring to a simmer over medium-high heat, then cover and reduce the heat to maintain a simmer. Cook until the apples are tender, about 15 minutes. Remove from the heat and, using a potato masher, mash into a coarse puree. Let the applesauce cool completely, then enjoy immediately or store in an airtight container in the refrigerator for up to 1 week.

HORSERADISH MAYO

Slather anything with mayo and I'll eat it. It's my ultimate condiment for sandwiches, burgers, and french fries, so I always have some on hand. And while a garlic or chipotle mayo never fails to get me going, whisking in a bit of the OG bitter herb has become my favorite variation. Adding grated fresh horseradish brings a sharp bite to mayo that just can't be matched (though you could substitute the jarred stuff if it's drained well). Yes, you could just stir it into store-bought mayo, but making it from scratch is so simple that you might as well break out the whisk.

YIELD: MAKES ABOUT 2 CUPS
PREP TIME: 10 MINUTES

2 large egg yolks, at room temperature

2 teaspoons kosher salt

1 teaspoon sugar

2 tablespoons freshly squeezed lemon juice

1 tablespoon white wine vinegar

2 cups vegetable oil

3 tablespoons finely grated fresh horseradish

1 In a heavy medium bowl, whisk the egg yolks, salt, and sugar until smooth. Slowly whisk in the lemon juice and vinegar until a thick paste forms.

2 While whisking continuously, slowly stream in the oil until a thick mayonnaise forms, then stir in the horseradish. Use immediately or store in an airtight container in the refrigerator for up to 2 weeks.

PICKLED ONIONS

While I'm not a connoisseur of half-sours, I'm all about making a jar of pickled red onions to always have on hand. Whether you need to add some bite to a bagel and lox, want to bump up the acid in a salad, or just need a bright topper for your morning avocado toast, there's never a wrong time for this beyond-simple fridge staple.

YIELD: MAKES ABOUT 2 CUPS
PREP TIME: 10 MINUTES, PLUS COOLING TIME
COOK TIME: 5 MINUTES

1 large red onion, thinly sliced

1 cup white wine vinegar

¼ cup sugar

1 tablespoon kosher salt

2 teaspoons coriander seeds

Pinch of crushed red pepper

Place the onion in a 24-ounce glass jar. In a small saucepan, combine the vinegar, sugar, salt, coriander, crushed red pepper, and 1 cup water and bring to a simmer over medium-high heat. Cook, stirring, until the sugar and salt have dissolved, about 2 minutes. Pour over the onion and let cool completely before sealing the jar. Store in the refrigerator for up to 2 weeks.

EVERYTHING SEASONING

This seasoning truly is everything. The combo of textures from sesame and poppy seeds is matched with the allium punch from dried flakes of garlic and onion to lift up any and every dish. Since we're making a seasoning and already using flaky sea salt, I veer from tradition and throw in some coarsely ground black pepper for just a little kick. Bagels are obviously at the top of the everything seasoning food pyramid, but don't hesitate to violently sprinkle this on avocado toast, soft-boiled eggs, roasted salmon, or even seared steak.

YIELD: MAKES ABOUT 1 CUP
PREP TIME: 5 MINUTES

¼ cup white sesame seeds, toasted
  (see tip, page 121)

¼ cup poppy seeds

3 tablespoons dried minced garlic

3 tablespoons dried minced onion

3 tablespoons flaky sea salt

1 tablespoon freshly ground black pepper

In a small airtight container, mix together the sesame seeds, poppy seeds, garlic, onion, salt, and pepper to combine. Store at room temperature for up to 1 month.

BAGEL CHIPS

Growing up, my mother always had a bag full of bagels in our freezer. She was really into the unusual-yet-life-changing combo of onion pumpernickel, but the bagel shop would only make them for her if she special-ordered at least two dozen at a time. As an adult who lives in NYC, my freezer remains bagel-free, given that a fresh one is only a block away. That being said, if I ever do have any leftover bagels, it's time for bagel chips. Much like pita chips, the bagel variety is just as sublime and oh-so-simple. I always have a bag in my pantry for scooping up any dip and, of course, for tossing into my Schmaltzy Chex Mix (page 56). You're going to be glad you got the baker's dozen.

YIELD: MAKES ABOUT 1 QUART
PREP TIME: 10 MINUTES, PLUS COOLING TIME
COOK TIME: 20 MINUTES

3 bagels, any flavor, sliced into
  ¼-inch-thick coins

¼ cup extra-virgin olive oil

½ teaspoon kosher salt

¼ teaspoon cayenne pepper

1 Preheat the oven to 350°F.

2 On a half sheet pan, toss the bagel coins, olive oil, salt, and cayenne to coat. Bake, tossing halfway through, for about 20 minutes, until golden brown and crisp. Let cool, then serve immediately or store in an airtight container at room temperature for up to 1 week.

CONCORD GRAPE AND MANISCHEWITZ JAM

If this book doesn't get me a Manischewitz sponsorship, I don't know what will. My love for the sugary Concord grape wine knows no bounds, so it was a natural progression to use it for making jam. It holds the most concentrated form of Concord grape flavor I think I'll ever experience, making it stunning when swirled into yogurt, iconic when piped into *sufganiyot* (page 227), and pretty damn flawless when slathered on that good ol' PB&J.

Some people get fancy when working with Concords, peeling them before pureeing the skins and seeding the pulp, but I have found success in laziness. I've always just thrown everything into a pot on the stove, and I'm not going to mess with a good thing.

If the thought of making jam sends you into a panic, know that you are seen. I'll walk you through how to tell when it's done so you don't end up with grape soup. The frozen-plate test in the instructions will be your best friend to see exactly when the jam is perfectly thickened. That's also why I throw in a bit of apple, since it won't add flavor, but it will fortify the mixture with an extra hit of pectin to help the jam set up when cooled.

YIELD: MAKES ABOUT 2½ CUPS
PREP TIME: 20 MINUTES, PLUS COOLING TIME AND OVERNIGHT CHILLING
COOK TIME: 45 MINUTES

2 pounds Concord grapes, stemmed (about 7 cups)

2 cups (400g) granulated sugar

2 cups Manischewitz wine

1 teaspoon kosher salt

½ Granny Smith apple, cored and coarsely chopped

2 tablespoons freshly squeezed lemon juice

1 Place a small plate in the freezer.

2 In a medium saucepan, combine the grapes, sugar, wine, salt, and apple. Bring to a light simmer over medium heat and cook, stirring occasionally, until the grapes and apple have broken down and the mixture has thickened so that when you scrape the bottom of the pan with a rubber spatula, the line it leaves behind holds its shape for a second before filling in, 45 to 55 minutes. To test if the jam is done, spoon ½ teaspoon of the jam onto the chilled plate and let sit for 1 minute, then tilt the plate. If the jam doesn't run, it's ready. If it runs, simmer the jam for a few minutes more and retest.

3 Remove from the heat and stir in the lemon juice. Strain the jam through a fine-mesh sieve, pressing gently on the solids with a rubber spatula until you've pushed through most of the pulp. You should have about ¼ cup of seeds and skins remaining in the sieve; discard them.

4 Transfer the jam to a 24-ounce glass jar and let cool completely before sealing. Refrigerate overnight before using, then store in the refrigerator for up to 2 months.

SCHUG (GREEN YEMENI HOT SAUCE)

Okay, so before we get into what this heavenly condiment really is, let's learn how to pronounce its name. Imagine how Nancy Gribble from *King of the Hill* calls everyone "shug," but replace the "h" with the guttural *ch* sound from challah. Boom, there you have it. As for what it is, *schug* is a fiery green hot sauce (though there are red versions, too) that was brought to Israel by Yemeni Jews. In addition to fresh chiles, this sauce is laden with tons of fresh cilantro and parsley for a brightness that you won't be able to find in any of the bottles of hot sauce at the back of your refrigerator. Serranos definitely bring the heat, but I'll let you be the master of your own domain in terms of quantity. To me, four chiles is the perfect number for a slow burn that builds up into the occasional single tear streaming down my cheek. However, power to you if you want to bring the pain with a few extra. While I will say that *schug* is especially good on my *Baharat* Smashed Potatoes (page 105), you really can't go wrong with having a jar of this on hand at all times. Stir it into your scrambled eggs! Throw it over grilled steak! Use it to marinate chicken! Eat it straight out of the jar like peanut butter! The possibilities are truly endless.

YIELD: MAKES ABOUT 2 CUPS
PREP TIME: 15 MINUTES

2 cups packed fresh parsley leaves and tender stems (1 bunch)

2 cups packed fresh cilantro leaves and tender stems (1 bunch)

2 teaspoons finely grated lemon zest

3 tablespoons freshly squeezed lemon juice

4 to 8 fresh serrano chiles, stemmed

4 garlic cloves, smashed and peeled

2 teaspoons kosher salt

½ teaspoon ground coriander

¼ teaspoon ground cumin

1 cup vegetable oil or grapeseed oil

In a food processor, combine the parsley, cilantro, lemon zest, lemon juice, chiles, garlic, salt, coriander, and cumin and pulse to chop. With the motor running, slowly stream in the oil until a semismooth sauce forms. Use immediately or store in an airtight container in the refrigerator for up to 2 weeks.

breakfast

Charred Scallion
Cream Cheese

YIELD: MAKES ABOUT 1 CUP

PREP TIME: 10 MINUTES

COOK TIME: 5 MINUTES

1 tablespoon extra-virgin olive oil

8 scallions

1 (8-ounce) package full-fat cream cheese, at room temperature

Kosher salt and freshly ground black pepper

Scallion cream cheese is the most important type of schmear, hands down. If I'm getting a bagel, I'm not asking for the regular stuff. I want the sharp, bright kick that you only get from a green-speckled, oniony cream cheese. To take that flavor to another level, charring the scallions quickly in a pan before slicing them and stirring them into the cream cheese imparts a hint of smokiness and a faint flavor of caramelized onions. It's the new best part of waking up.

1 Heat a large cast-iron pan over high heat. Add the olive oil, followed by the scallions, and cook, turning them as needed, until lightly charred, 3 to 4 minutes. Transfer to a cutting board and let cool slightly, then finely chop.

2 In a medium bowl, stir together the scallions and cream cheese until well incorporated. Season with salt and pepper. Use immediately or refrigerate in an airtight container at room temperature for up to 1 week.

the anatomy
of the
perfect bagel

Now that you've got the best schmear recipe on the market, let's break down what to serve it with. (Plus, don't forget to finish it with flaky sea salt and a squeeze of lemon for a little hit of acid.)

Tomatoes: Thickly sliced, and if it's summer, they better be heirloom.

Capers: Sprinkled over the cream cheese so they stick instead of falling off.

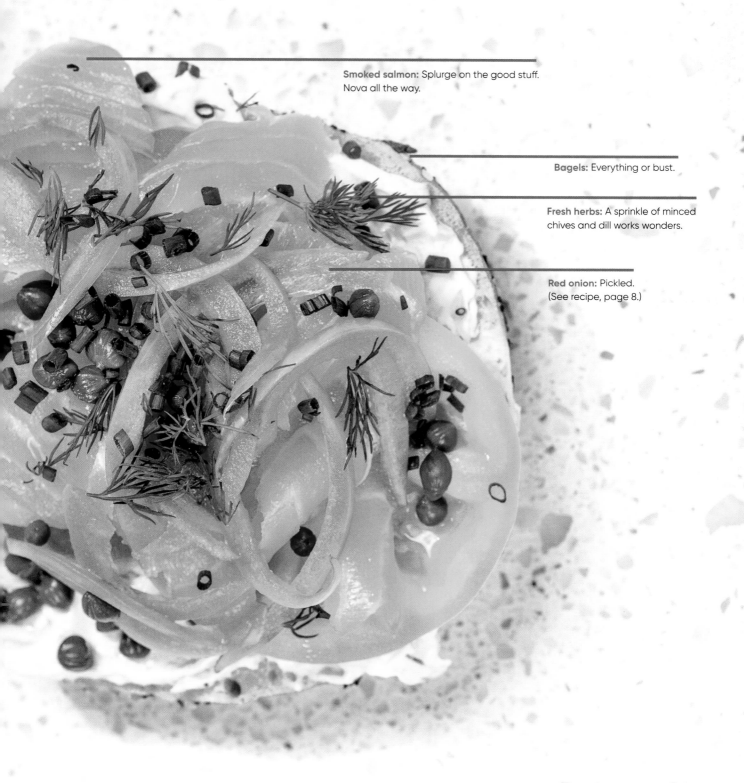

Smoked salmon: Splurge on the good stuff. Nova all the way.

Bagels: Everything or bust.

Fresh herbs: A sprinkle of minced chives and dill works wonders.

Red onion: Pickled. (See recipe, page 8.)

Sabich Bagel Sandwiches

YIELD: MAKES 8 SANDWICHES

PREP TIME: 30 MINUTES

COOK TIME: 20 MINUTES

FOR THE AMBA-TAHINI CREAM CHEESE

2 (8-ounce) packages full-fat cream cheese, at room temperature

¼ cup amba (see page 4)

¼ cup tahini

Kosher salt

FOR THE EGGPLANT AND EGGS

1 large eggplant, cut into ¼-inch-thick rounds

Kosher salt

¾ cup extra-virgin olive oil

8 large eggs

FOR THE BAGEL SANDWICHES

8 sesame bagels, split open and lightly toasted

2 beefsteak tomatoes, thinly sliced

½ English cucumber, thinly sliced on an angle

1 small red onion, thinly sliced into rings

Sliced Middle Eastern pickles, for serving (optional)

If you love geeking out over the magic of Jewish Diaspora dishes and Israeli cuisine, you're going to love *sabich!* Oh, and if you love eggs and eggplant and anything with tahini, you'll probably love *sabich*, too. When Iraqi Jews brought to Israel their breakfast of hard-boiled eggs, fried eggplant, and *amba*, a spicy pickled mango sauce, it quickly got absorbed into the culinary canon. Only labeled *"sabich"* when stuffed into a pita pocket in the Promised Land, this dish is one of the most satisfying ways to start the day.

It's pretty tricky to make at home for the sole reason that quality pita is just not widely available in the States. But do you know what is? Top-shelf bagels! I swap the vessel to give you the same flavors with a New York–Ashkenazi spin. The *amba* and tahini get swirled into cream cheese for a rich schmear that brings nutty and spicy tones. The tomato-cucumber salad is swapped with sliced tomato, cukes, and red onion, which is so much easier to prepare. The hard-boiled eggs are replaced with fried eggs for a little yolk porn to smother the fried eggplant. It's a two-hand breakfast that's truly unlike any bagel creation you've ever had.

1 For the amba-tahini cream cheese: In a medium bowl, stir together the cream cheese, amba, and tahini until smooth and well incorporated. Season with salt.

2 For the eggplant and eggs: Line a plate with paper towels. In a large bowl, toss the eggplant with a heavy pinch of salt.

3 In a large nonstick skillet, heat 3 tablespoons of the olive oil over medium-high heat. Add 5 or 6 of the eggplant slices and fry, flipping once, until golden brown, about 2 minutes per side. Transfer to the paper towels to drain. Repeat to cook the remaining eggplant, working in two more batches and heating 3 tablespoons of the oil in the skillet before each batch.

4 In the same skillet, heat the remaining 3 tablespoons oil over medium-high heat. Crack in 4 of the eggs and season each with a pinch of salt. Cook until the whites have just set, 3 to 4 minutes. Transfer to a plate and repeat with the remaining 4 eggs.

5 For the bagel sandwiches: Onto the bottom half of each bagel, schmear some of the amba-tahini cream cheese, then divide the fried eggplant, tomato, cucumber, onion, eggs, and pickles (if using) evenly among them. Spread some of the amba-tahini cream cheese on the other half of each bagel, then sandwich and serve.

Pie Crust 101. Chill out. You need all your ingredients as cold as possible. That way, you'll have more visible chunks of butter throughout the dough. As it bakes, each butter pocket melts and steams, creating the flaky layers you want.

Pour it up! Here, as in most times in life, vodka is your friend! Using alcohol in your dough not only helps it come together, but inhibits gluten development for a more tender crust.

Get stoned. Pizza stoned, that is. If you have a pizza stone or baking steel, bake your galette on it to help ensure a super-crisp and golden bottom crust.

Everything Bagel Galette

YIELD: SERVES 8 TO 10

PREP TIME: 30 MINUTES, PLUS 1 HOUR CHILLING TIME

COOK TIME: 50 MINUTES

FOR THE DOUGH

3 cups (405g) all-purpose flour, plus more for dusting

1 teaspoon kosher salt

8 ounces (2 sticks) unsalted butter, frozen

½ cup plus 2 tablespoons ice-cold water

2 tablespoons ice-cold vodka

FOR THE FILLING AND ASSEMBLY

1 (8-ounce) package full-fat cream cheese, at room temperature

1 tablespoon drained capers, minced

2 teaspoons finely grated lemon zest

1½ teaspoons kosher salt

4 scallions, thinly sliced, plus more sliced scallion greens for garnish

8 ounces sliced Nova smoked salmon

4 medium heirloom tomatoes, sliced ¼ inch thick

1 large egg, beaten

1 tablespoon Everything Seasoning (page 9)

Flaky sea salt, for garnish

Fresh dill fronds, for garnish

Heirloom tomato season may be one of the most magical times of the year. It's the only time that tomatoes actually taste as they should, and I ignore my acid reflux to slice and dice them to serve on anything and everything in celebration. I decided to Frankenstein the classic bagel and lox with my obsession for heirloom tomato galettes into the mash-up nobody asked for but everybody needs.

The first time I tested this, my brother-in-law Manuel ate three-quarters of the whole galette, proclaiming with excitement and finesse that it has "all of the flavors," which has now become the way I best describe this recipe. If you think about it, it's like serving a giant, sliceable everything bagel for a crowd by wrapping up scallion cream cheese, cured salmon, and juicy heirloom tomato slices in a flaky all-butter crust. As it bakes, the juices of the jammy caramelized tomatoes trickle down to each layer and the flavors infuse into a free-form pie of concentrated Judaism.

1 For the dough (see tips, opposite): In a large bowl, whisk together the flour and kosher salt. Using a box grater, coarsely grate the frozen butter, then add it to the flour mixture and toss to coat. Add the water and vodka and hand knead the mixture until a shaggy dough forms. Cover the dough with plastic wrap and refrigerate for 1 hour.

2 For the filling and assembly: In a medium bowl, stir together the cream cheese, capers, lemon zest, 1 teaspoon of the kosher salt, and the scallions until incorporated.

3 Preheat the oven to 400°F. Line a half sheet pan with parchment paper.

4 On a lightly floured surface, roll out the dough into an 18-inch round, ⅛ inch thick. Transfer the dough to the prepared sheet pan. Spread the cream cheese mixture over the dough in an even layer, leaving a 2-inch border. Layer the smoked salmon over the cream cheese, followed by the tomato slices, shingling them to cover the cream cheese. Season the tomatoes with the remaining ½ teaspoon kosher salt.

5 Fold the exposed border of the dough over the tomatoes with a series of pleats, then brush the outside of the dough liberally with the beaten egg and sprinkle with the everything seasoning.

6 Bake for 50 to 60 minutes, until the crust is golden brown. Let cool for about 15 minutes, until just warm.

7 Top the galette with a pinch of flaky sea salt, sliced scallions, and dill. Slice and serve.

Shakshuka alla Vodka

YIELD: SERVES 4 TO 6
PREP TIME: 15 MINUTES
COOK TIME: 30 MINUTES

2 tablespoons extra-virgin olive oil

2 garlic cloves, thinly sliced

1 medium yellow onion, finely chopped

1 teaspoon ground cumin

½ teaspoon crushed red pepper

¼ cup vodka

1 (15-ounce) can tomato puree

1 (14½-ounce) can fire-roasted diced tomatoes

¾ cup full-fat sour cream

Kosher salt and freshly ground black pepper

6 large eggs

2 tablespoons chopped fresh parsley

Warm pita or toasted challah, for serving

Yet another gorgeous addition to Israeli cuisine brought over from the Sephardic Jews of North Africa, shakshuka is one of the easiest and most satisfying egg dishes in the world. A vibrant tomato sauce is cooked down until it's thick enough to cradle and poach eggs to finish this one-skillet sensation that's begging to be scooped up by tons of warm pita or toasted challah.

Naturally, I had to take something perfectly good and mash it up with something just as comforting! Say what you want about penne alla vodka, but I'm a big fan, and I'm absolutely obsessed with using a vodka sauce for this shakshuka. It all comes down to science and not my childlike palate. With most of the vodka cooked off, the trace amounts of alcohol in the sauce help amplify aromas and bring out flavors you otherwise wouldn't experience. Of course, the addition of sour cream for richness is pretty nice, too. Throw in a few eggs, and you're left with a dish that's perfect for any brunch blowout or breakfast-for-dinner situation.

1 In a large skillet, heat the olive oil over medium-high heat. Add the garlic and onion and cook, stirring often, until softened and lightly caramelized, 6 to 8 minutes. Stir in the cumin and crushed red pepper and cook until fragrant, about 1 minute.

2 Reduce the heat to medium, then add the vodka, immediately followed by the tomato puree and diced tomatoes. Bring to a light simmer and cook, stirring occasionally, until slightly thickened, about 15 minutes. Stir in the sour cream, then season with salt and black pepper.

3 Using a wooden spoon, make six wells in the sauce and crack an egg into each well. Season each egg with a pinch of salt, then cover and cook until the whites are just set, 3 to 4 minutes.

4 Remove from the heat and garnish with the parsley. Serve with warm pita or toasted challah.

Persian-ish
Kuku Quiche

YIELD: SERVES 10 TO 12

PREP TIME: 30 MINUTES, PLUS 1 HOUR
CHILLING TIME AND COOLING TIME

COOK TIME: 1 HOUR 30 MINUTES

I'm all about pie for breakfast, so you better believe I love a good slice of quiche to start my day. Add the fact that you can make it in advance and serve it at room temperature, and you've got a damn near perfect brunch dish, and one that I frequently turn to for morning entertaining. This variation takes inspiration from *kuku sabzi,* a Persian green-herb omelet that's really more herbs than eggs. With tons of chopped parsley, cilantro, dill, and scallions, it's packed with enough greens to balance a super-buttery and flaky crust. Since this recipe already veers so far from tradition, I top the whole thing off with crumbles of goat cheese to add some tang. It's so quiche!

The most important part of making a quiche is blind baking your crust. This is the process of baking the unfilled bottom crust for a bit before adding the filling to ensure golden and flaky layers in your finished product. To do so, you line the pie dough with parchment paper or aluminum foil, then fill it with pie weights, which can be anything from fancy ceramic balls to the more commonly used dried beans or uncooked rice. This prevents the crust from sagging in the oven before it's set, and once it is, you pull out the weights and continue baking the crust until lightly golden all over. The beauty of using a glass pie plate is that throughout the whole process, you can just pick it up to peek at the bottom to ensure it's golden.

RECIPE CONTINUES

FOR THE CRUST

1½ cups (205g) all-purpose flour, plus more for dusting

1 teaspoon kosher salt

4 ounces (1 stick) unsalted butter, frozen

¼ cup ice-cold water

2 tablespoons plain full-fat yogurt

FOR THE FILLING

6 large eggs

1¼ cups half-and-half

1 cup packed fresh parsley leaves and tender stems, coarsely chopped

1 cup packed fresh dill fronds and tender stems, coarsely chopped

1 cup packed fresh cilantro leaves and tender stems, coarsely chopped

1 teaspoon kosher salt

1 teaspoon finely grated lemon zest

¼ teaspoon crushed red pepper

4 scallions, thinly sliced

4 ounces goat cheese, crumbled

1 teaspoon ground sumac, for garnish (optional)

1 For the crust (see tips, page 20): In a large bowl, whisk together the flour and salt. Using a box grater, coarsely grate the frozen butter, then add it to the flour mixture and toss to coat. Add the water and yogurt and knead the mixture with your hands until a shaggy dough forms. Cover the dough with plastic wrap and refrigerate for 1 hour.

2 Preheat the oven to 400°F.

3 On a lightly floured surface, roll out the dough into a 12-inch round, ⅛ inch thick. Drape the dough over a 9-inch glass pie dish, adjusting it so the dough is flush with the surface, then trim any overhanging dough with a paring knife or kitchen shears. Crimp the crust by using your fingers to make a series of pinches around the edges of the dough. Place the pie dish on a half sheet pan. Line the dough with parchment paper or aluminum foil, being sure to have at least 2 inches of overhang all around, then fill the parchment or foil with pie weights, dried beans, or uncooked rice up to the crimped edges of the dough.

4 Bake for 25 to 30 minutes, until the bottom of the dough is beginning to turn golden. Remove from the oven and carefully transfer the pie weights to a heatproof bowl to cool; discard the parchment or foil. Return the crust to the oven and bake for 10 to 15 minutes more, until evenly golden. Remove from the oven and let cool. Reduce the oven temperature to 325°F.

5 For the filling: Meanwhile, in a large bowl, beat the eggs until smooth, then whisk in the half-and-half, parsley, dill, cilantro, salt, lemon zest, crushed red pepper, and scallions.

6 Pour the filling into the cooled pie crust and top with the goat cheese. Bake for 50 to 60 minutes, until the eggs are just set and don't jiggle when the pie dish is gently shaken. Remove from the oven and let cool completely.

7 Garnish with the sumac, if desired, then slice and serve.

Rose Water and Cardamom French Toast

YIELD: SERVES 6 TO 8

PREP TIME: 15 MINUTES, PLUS 1 HOUR
SOAKING TIME

COOK TIME: 20 MINUTES

3 cups whole milk

½ cup sugar

1½ tablespoons rose water

1 teaspoon kosher salt

¾ teaspoon ground cardamom

6 large eggs

1 (16-ounce) loaf challah bread
   (see page xvii), sliced 1 inch thick

6 tablespoons (¾ stick) unsalted butter

Dried food-grade rose petals, for
   garnish (optional)

Maple syrup, for serving

It's Shabbat tradition to always have two challahs on the table. While the real reason is to represent abundance, I like to say its purpose is to have one left over for French toast the next morning. Funny story: Alex stood me up on our second date, for which I had prepared a brunch spread including a huge platter of challah French toast that I proceeded to eat alone on my couch in disappointment. Love wins!

Naturally, you already know that it all worked out for us, and French toast has become an integral part of our relationship. Over the years, I've tried to switch it up past the expected flavorings of vanilla and cinnamon. Instead, I go the Middle Eastern route, adding floral rose water and warm cardamom to the mix. (For those of you who love rose water as much as we do, try spiking your maple syrup with a splash for an extra kick of floral sweetness.)

Now, the secret to achieving the custardy French toast of your dreams is making sure the bread soaks long enough. You want each piece to be completely saturated in the egg mixture before slowly frying them in butter to fully cook the centers. All that's left is to platter them up and pray your breakfast guest(s) arrive. If not, you've luckily discovered the beauty of meal planning and now will be enjoying this recipe every morning for the rest of the week!

1 In a large bowl, whisk together the milk, sugar, rose water, salt, cardamom, and eggs until smooth.

2 Arrange the challah slices over the bottom of a large baking dish, shingling them to fit, then pour over the milk mixture. Cover with plastic wrap and refrigerate for 1 hour to soak.

3 In a large nonstick skillet, melt 1 tablespoon of the butter over medium heat. Add about 3 slices of the soaked challah to the pan and cook until golden, 2 to 3 minutes. Flip the challah, add another tablespoon of the butter to the pan, and cook until golden and cooked through, 2 minutes more. Transfer the French toast to a platter. Repeat to cook the remaining soaked challah slices, working in two batches and using the remaining butter.

4 Garnish the French toast with a pinch of dried rose petals, if desired, then serve immediately with maple syrup.

Citrus and Poppy Seed Pancakes

YIELD: SERVES 6 TO 8

PREP TIME: 25 MINUTES

COOK TIME: 20 MINUTES

FOR THE PANCAKES

½ cup poppy seeds

6 tablespoons (75g) sugar

1 teaspoon kosher salt

Finely grated zest of 1 orange

Finely grated zest of 1 lemon

Finely grated zest of 1 lime

2 cups buttermilk

2 cups whole milk

4 large eggs

4 cups (540g) all-purpose flour

2 tablespoons baking soda

2 tablespoons baking powder

Nonstick cooking spray, for greasing

FOR THE LEMON-LIME CREAM

1 cup full-fat sour cream

2 tablespoons sugar

1½ tablespoons freshly squeezed
lemon juice

1½ tablespoons freshly squeezed
lime juice

½ teaspoon kosher salt

FOR SERVING

Orange segments

Mixed berries

Maple syrup

There's no better way to show friends or family how much you love them first thing in the morning than flipping fluffy flapjacks directly onto their plates. While there is always a time and place for chocolate chip smiley-faces, these pancakes take sweet inspiration from some of my other favorite desserts I want to be eating for breakfast. Ground poppy seeds, the superstar of Eastern European Jewish confections (and my favorite hamantaschen flavor), add wonderful texture with a nutty and slightly fruity flavor, especially when paired with a trio of citrus zests. I find that adding this combination of lemon, lime, and orange zests to any batter gives it a whimsical brightness that falls somewhere in flavor between birthday cake and a Flintstones push-pop (the OG ice cream truck sensation).

For me, perfect pancakes are nothing more than this ratio of flour, eggs, buttermilk, and leaveners. That means after you fall in love with this recipe, you can continue to ignite your passion for pancakes in any way that doesn't mess with my ratio, like studding each scoop of batter with blueberries, swapping out citrus for warm baking spices, or even folding in chopped nuts in lieu of the poppy seeds.

As for the lemon-lime cream, it's my way to use up the zested lemon and lime and make a topping that gives citrus curd vibes without having to whip out the double boiler. For serving, I recommend setting up a toppings bar on the table with the lemon-lime cream, orange segments, berries, and a hefty pitcher of maple syrup. Oh, and mimosas. I recommend serving tons of mimosas, which might be the most important accouterment.

1 For the pancakes: In a blender, combine the poppy seeds, sugar, salt, orange zest, lemon zest, and lime zest and blend on high until the seeds are coarsely ground, 1 to 2 minutes. Add the buttermilk, whole milk, and eggs and blend until smooth.

2 In a large bowl, whisk together the flour, baking soda, and baking powder. Fold in the buttermilk mixture until just incorporated.

3 Heat two medium nonstick skillets over medium heat. Spray each liberally with cooking spray, then spoon ½ cup of the batter into each pan. Cook the pancakes, flipping them once, until golden brown and puffed, 1 to 2 minutes per side. Transfer the pancakes to a platter and repeat, spraying the pans with more cooking spray as needed between batches, until you've used up all of the batter (you should have about 16 pancakes).

4 For the lemon-lime cream: In a small bowl, whisk together the sour cream, sugar, lemon juice, lime juice, and salt until smooth.

5 Divide the pancakes among serving plates and top with the lemon-lime cream, orange segments, and mixed berries, then serve with maple syrup.

Pastrami Biscuits and Gravy

YIELD: SERVES 6 TO 8

PREP TIME: 45 MINUTES, PLUS 30 MINUTES
CHILLING TIME

COOK TIME: 35 MINUTES

FOR THE BISCUITS

5 cups (675g) all-purpose flour

2½ tablespoons baking powder

1 tablespoon coriander seeds, toasted
and coarsely ground

1 tablespoon whole black peppercorns,
coarsely ground

1 tablespoon packed light brown sugar

1 tablespoon kosher salt

1 teaspoon baking soda

1 teaspoon garlic powder

1 teaspoon onion powder

1 teaspoon sweet paprika

1 pound 2 ounces (4½ sticks) unsalted
butter, 4 sticks frozen, ½ stick melted

2 cups buttermilk, cold

Flaky sea salt and freshly ground black
pepper, for garnish

FOR THE GRAVY

4 tablespoons (½ stick) unsalted butter

12 ounces thick-cut pastrami, diced

1 garlic clove, minced

¼ cup (34g) all-purpose flour

2½ cups whole milk

¼ cup minced fresh chives, plus more for
garnish

1 tablespoon maple syrup

Kosher salt and freshly ground black
pepper

I may not be Southern, but I sure make one hell of a biscuit. It all started when I tested Nancy Silverton's all-butter biscuits for *Saveur* and fell in love with her techniques of laminating the dough and cutting square biscuits. Years of tweaking and prodding my recipe have brought me here, with the fluffiest, flakiest creation you'll ever find. A buttermilk dough packed with a full pound of grated frozen butter (I hand-grate it, but you can definitely use your food processor's grating attachment) is folded onto itself to ensure little layers of butter throughout each biscuit, ready to bake into flaky pockets.

Yes, these biscuits are great on their own. But now imagine them covered in a rich pastrami gravy! It's the same idea as sausage gravy, but with Jewish deli. To amp up the pastrami vibes, the biscuits themselves are studded with the same spices you would find in pastrami seasoning, like black pepper and coriander. I'm begging you to invest in a spice grinder or mortar and pestle so you'll be able to coarsely grind freshly toasted coriander seeds and black peppercorns. If you're really in a pinch without either tool for grinding, you can empty a pepper mill and throw in the coriander to MacGyver the situation.

If you're feeling wild, throw a fried egg on top of this masterpiece, and you've got yourself an indulgent breakfast best enjoyed wearing pants with an elastic waist.

1 For the biscuits: Preheat the oven to 400°F. Line two half sheet pans with parchment paper.

2 In a large bowl, whisk together the flour, baking powder, coriander, pepper, brown sugar, kosher salt, baking soda, garlic powder, onion powder, and paprika to combine.

3 Using a box grater, coarsely grate the 4 sticks of frozen butter, then add it to the flour mixture and toss to coat. Add the buttermilk and, using your hands, knead until a shaggy dough forms.

4 Transfer the dough to a clean work surface and knead until smooth. Shape the dough into a rectangle and lightly dust it with flour. Roll the dough into a 9 by 12-inch rectangle, then fold it into thirds like a letter. Dust the dough with more flour and rotate it 90 degrees. Repeat this process of rolling out and folding the dough twice more, rotating after each fold, for a total of three folds.

5 Roll the dough out into a 9 by 12-inch rectangle, aligned horizontally,

RECIPE CONTINUES

and trim the outer ¼ inch to create clean edges. Cut the dough into 3 rows and 4 columns to form 12 equal squares. Transfer the biscuits to one of the prepared sheet pans and refrigerate for 30 minutes.

6 Transfer half the biscuits to the other prepared pan. Space the biscuits on both pans 2 inches apart. Brush the melted butter liberally on the biscuits and garnish each with a pinch each of flaky sea salt and pepper.

7 Bake, rotating the pans halfway through, for 25 to 30 minutes, until the biscuits have risen and are golden brown.

8 For the gravy: In a medium saucepan, melt 2 tablespoons of the butter over medium-high heat. Add the pastrami and garlic and cook, stirring often, until lightly golden, 3 to 4 minutes. Using a slotted spoon, transfer the pastrami and garlic to a bowl.

9 In the same pan, melt the remaining 2 tablespoons butter, then add the flour and cook, stirring with a wooden spoon, until blond in color, 1 to 2 minutes. Slowly whisk in the milk until smooth, then cook, stirring continuously, until thickened, about 5 minutes. Stir in the pastrami, chives, and maple syrup, then season with salt and pepper.

10 Serve the biscuits warm, with the gravy and a garnishing of chives for topping.

Caramel Apple Sticky Buns

YIELD: MAKES 12 STICKY BUNS

PREP TIME: 30 MINUTES, PLUS 2 HOURS 15 MINUTES PROOFING TIME

COOK TIME: 40 MINUTES

FOR THE DOUGH

1 cup whole milk, heated to 115°F

½ cup (100g) granulated sugar

1 (¼-ounce) packet active dry yeast (2¼ teaspoons)

2 large eggs

4 ounces (1 stick) unsalted butter, melted

4½ cups (608g) all-purpose flour

¼ cup packed (50g) dark brown sugar

1 teaspoon kosher salt

2 tablespoons vegetable oil, for greasing

FOR THE STICKY STUFF AND FILLING

4 ounces (1 stick) unsalted butter, melted

1½ cups packed (300g) dark brown sugar

⅓ cup honey

1 teaspoon kosher salt

½ cup apple butter

2 tablespoons ground cinnamon

2 Honeycrisp apples, peeled, cored, and finely chopped

Fall baking is my favorite national pastime, and the fact that it overlaps with the Jewish High Holidays typically means that my oven is always on. These sticky buns are a product of autumnal weekend getaways to the Hudson Valley in New York where my husband and I put on our coziest turtlenecks and head to a local farm to pick a bushel of apples for me to play with, since naturally our Airbnb is chosen based on the kitchen. Inspired by constant visits to Bread Alone Bakery for their sticky buns and sweets, I fused the pastry with the Rosh Hashanah motif of apples and honey to create a marginally healthier take on the breakfast treat. Between the combo of fresh apples and apple butter that melts into the warm, fluffy buns and the honey caramel that saturates the whole dish, this recipe is a cinnamon-scented alarm clock that will wake up the whole house.

As I write this, I can hear my mother in the back of my head, guilting me for not adding nuts to these buns, since she would like just about any baked good that comes out of my oven to be studded with walnuts. Listen, if you're so inclined, you can chop up a cup of walnuts or pecans to sprinkle over the filling before you roll up the dough. However, sticky buns are one of the few things that I do not need textural contrast with, so I'm not going to mess with a good thing. I just think it's more important to stress that I don't want none unless you got buns, hun.

1 For the dough: In the bowl of a stand mixer fitted with the whisk attachment, whisk together the milk and granulated sugar. Sprinkle the yeast over the top and let stand until foamy, 5 to 10 minutes. With the mixer running on medium speed, add the eggs, followed by the melted butter, and mix until well incorporated. Switch to the dough hook, then add the flour, brown sugar, and salt to the bowl. Beginning on low speed and gradually increasing to medium, knead until a smooth, elastic dough forms, about 5 minutes.

2 Grease a medium bowl and your hands with the oil. Using your hands, transfer the dough to the bowl, gently turning it to coat it with the oil and shape it into a smooth ball. Cover with plastic wrap or a clean kitchen towel and set aside in a warm place until doubled in size, about 1 hour 30 minutes.

RECIPE CONTINUES

3 For the sticky stuff and filling: In a medium bowl, stir together the melted butter, brown sugar, honey, and salt until smooth. Spread half of this mixture evenly over the bottom of a 9 by 13-inch baking pan. Add the apple butter and cinnamon to the brown sugar mixture remaining in the bowl and stir until well incorporated.

4 Once the dough has risen, transfer it to a lightly floured surface. Roll it out into a 12 by 18-inch rectangle, about ½ inch thick, aligned horizontally. Spread the apple butter mixture in an even layer over the dough, leaving a 1-inch border at the top, then sprinkle the apples over the apple butter mixture. Starting with the edge closest to you, roll up the dough tightly, then slice it crosswise into 12 (1½-inch-thick) disks. Place them cut-side down in the prepared baking pan. Cover with plastic wrap or a clean kitchen towel and set aside in a warm place, until they've puffed to fill out the pan, 45 minutes to 1 hour.

5 Meanwhile, preheat the oven to 350°F.

6 Bake the sticky buns for 40 to 45 minutes, until golden brown and risen. Remove from the oven and let cool in the pan for 10 minutes. Place a platter over the baking pan and invert them together, then remove the pan to reveal the sticky buns. Serve warm.

Challah Croque Monsieurs

YIELD: MAKES 6 SANDWICHES

PREP TIME: 15 MINUTES, PLUS COOLING TIME

COOK TIME: 30 MINUTES

2 cups coarsely grated Gruyère cheese

1 cup coarsely grated Parmesan cheese

4 tablespoons (½ stick) unsalted butter

¼ cup (34g) all-purpose flour

3 cups whole milk

2 garlic cloves, finely grated

1 sprig sage

1 sprig thyme

1 sprig rosemary

1 teaspoon finely grated lemon zest

Pinch of freshly grated nutmeg (optional)

Kosher salt and freshly ground black pepper

12 (¾-inch-thick) slices challah bread (page xvii) from 1 large loaf

12 thick-cut slices honey-baked ham or smoked turkey

Let's be real, a croque monsieur is the ultimate brunch crowd-pleaser. It's an easy, cheesy French sandwich that tastes like a warm hug to your arteries! I've played around with bread from sourdough to brioche, but simply nothing beats using challah. Its sweetness balances the salty richness of the cheese, while its soft texture is perfect for soaking up all that dreamy béchamel. Turning leftover loaves into a weekend-brunch powerhouse, this version packs in ham (I'm sorry!!) or smoked turkey, though if you're looking to keep things kosher, play around with roasted veggies or sautéed mushrooms. Any route you go, I highly recommend you throw a fried egg on top for the sexiest croque madame you ever did see.

1 Preheat the oven to 400°F. Line a half sheet pan with parchment paper.

2 In a small bowl, toss together the Gruyère and Parmesan to combine.

3 In a medium saucepan, melt the butter over medium heat. Add the flour and cook, stirring continuously with a wooden spoon, until blond in color, about 2 minutes. Slowly whisk in the milk until smooth, then add the garlic, sage, thyme, and rosemary. Bring to a simmer and cook, stirring often, until thickened, about 5 minutes. Remove from the heat and stir in half the grated cheeses, the lemon zest, and the nutmeg (if using). Season with salt and pepper. Let the béchamel sauce cool, then discard the herbs.

4 Spread 2 tablespoons of the béchamel on both sides of 6 slices of the challah and place them on the prepared sheet pan. Layer each with 2 slices of the ham (or turkey) and 2 tablespoons of the grated cheeses. Spread 2 tablespoons of the béchamel on both sides of the remaining 6 slices of challah and place them over the cheese to close the sandwiches. Top with any remaining béchamel and the remaining grated cheeses.

5 Bake for 20 to 25 minutes, until golden and bubbling. Serve immediately.

Persian-ish Granola

YIELD: MAKES 6 CUPS
PREP TIME: 20 MINUTES, PLUS COOLING TIME
COOK TIME: 25 MINUTES

3 cups rolled oats

½ cup pine nuts

½ cup raw pistachios

½ cup pitted Deglet Noor dates, coarsely chopped

½ cup dried currants

⅓ cup pistachio oil or melted coconut oil

¼ cup date syrup (silan) or maple syrup

¼ cup packed (50g) light brown sugar

2 tablespoons rose water

2 teaspoons ground cinnamon

1 teaspoon kosher salt

½ teaspoon ground cloves

½ teaspoon ground cardamom

After all of the oohs and ahhs when my mother-in-law, Robina, flips out a perfect *tahdig* (see page 132), she tops the rice with fried currants and pine nuts that have been perfumed with spices like cinnamon, cardamom, and clove. It's not a traditional topping to Persian rice, but an addition that brings in elements of her Iraqi heritage and time living in Turkey. Every time Robina makes it, I can't help myself from eating handfuls of the currant mixture straight from the top of the crust. Between the combo of crunchy and chewy textures, the hint of sweetness, and the warmth from the spices, it's like Middle Eastern trail mix, so it wasn't a far stretch to want to develop a granola recipe with the same vibes.

To make it worthy of the most important meal of the day, the same combo of pine nuts, currants, and warm spices is mixed with oats, pistachios, and chopped dates before getting baked into golden clusters. I'm a firm believer in making batches of granola that I won't finish in one sitting, so this recipe yields enough to keep you topping your morning yogurt for a while.

1 Preheat the oven to 350°F. Line a half sheet pan with parchment paper.

2 In a large bowl, toss together the oats, pine nuts, pistachios, dates, and currants to combine.

3 In a medium bowl, whisk together the pistachio oil, date syrup, brown sugar, rose water, cinnamon, salt, cloves, and cardamom until smooth, then pour over the oat mixture and

toss to coat. Transfer the mixture to the prepared sheet pan and spread it into an even layer.

4 Bake the granola, stirring once halfway through, for 25 to 30 minutes, until golden and crisp. Remove from the oven and let cool completely, then stir to break up the granola clusters into smaller pieces. Serve, or store in an airtight container at room temperature for up to 1 month.

HIGH HOLIDAYS OF OUR LIVES

First time hosting? Tasked with bringing a dessert and want to show up your cousins? Meeting your Jewish in-laws for the first time? I got you covered with some curated menus.

rosh hashanah

New year, same Jew. Let's sweeten it up a bit!

———

apps + snacks

The Art of the Cheese Board

Y ou may think a voluptuous cheese board is just a way I try to show off how much of a fancy host I am, which is a valid statement, but its true purpose is to buy me time. A curated board of dairy creates a delicious distraction for my guests to fawn over while I get everything cooking or reheating for the main event. The night before the first Shabbat meal I hosted a few years back, I ran to Murray's Cheese to pick up a spread of triple-creams, ash rinds, and funky blues to cover a wooden board adorned with fresh honeycomb, plump green olives, and at least three types of crackers. As soon as that first board was served, 'grammed, and destroyed, in that order, it became a signature feature at any gathering I hosted, growing in size with the guest list. No matter how big or small, bougie or simple, kosher or treif, I've got some guidelines for a picture-perfect cheese board that's sure to blow your guests away.

Lots of cheese: When I host twelve people for Shabbat, I try to pick four or five cheeses for a board, aiming at around 8 ounces of each. Typically I choose one soft-ripened cheese (like Brie or ash-rind goat's cheese), one semi-firm (like Gruyère or cheddar), one firm (like Manchego or aged Gouda), one blue (like Roquefort or Stilton), and one surprise cheese that might be a little funkier or out there in flavor to spice things up.

Something meaty: You do you! If you don't do pork, sliced beef salami or bresaola does the trick. If you don't mix meat and dairy, omit the meat altogether. If you don't let kosher law dictate your diet or Jewish identity (that's me), ball out with whatever you like. I try to add on one sliced salami and 4 to 8 ounces of sliced prosciutto or jamón, but I'm a sucker for throwing in some mortadella, too.

Something pickled: With so much cheese, you need something briny to help cut through all that richness. I love a cornichon moment, but nowadays it has become so easy to find a rainbow of pickles like green beans, okra, spicy peppers, and carrots to add some extra color and texture. As for the olives, it's all about the Castelvetrano. They're big and meaty and the perfect gateway olive for someone who says they don't like olives. The only thing to note is that if your olives aren't pitted, make sure to put out a little bowl where your guests can discard their pits.

Something sweet: I crave something sweet to pair with luscious Brie or funky blue. Start to explore the treacly world of honey, which varies greatly in color, thickness, and flavor. I tend to always serve a bowl of honey as well as fresh honeycomb, which adds a bit of texture with sweetness. But don't stop there—dried and fresh fruit are another great way to sneak in some extra sweetness and a subtle veil of healthiness. Think seasonally with berries, stone fruit, grapes, and apples on rotation, as well as dried dates, apricots, cranberries, and figs to complement.

Something nutty: I'm always in the mood for salty nuts, and a cheese board is no exception. They bridge many of the toasty, nutty flavors of the cheeses, as well as adding crunch to provide some textural contrast. Go nuts with piles of toasted cashews, pistachios, Marcona almonds, or candied walnuts.

Something to hold it all together: What would all this beauty be without a vessel to shovel it into your mouth? I like variety with my crackers, typically always throwing on some sea salt Firehook crackers, paired

with anything packed with dried fruit and nuts like Raincoast Crisps. Switch it up with whatever flavors and textures meet your fancy, and that means the occasional add-on of freshly sliced baguette or a swap-in of matzo for Pesach.

Roasted Garlic Hummus

YIELD: MAKES ABOUT 5 CUPS

PREP TIME: 10 MINUTES

COOK TIME: 1 HOUR

2 tablespoons extra-virgin olive oil

1 head garlic, halved crosswise

2 (15½-ounce) cans chickpeas

½ cup tahini

⅓ cup freshly squeezed lemon juice

Kosher salt

Pita and crudités, for serving

Somewhere in Philadelphia, Mike Solomonov is unfollowing me on Instagram as he reads that my hummus recipe uses canned chickpeas. But before you turn the page, let me plead my case for my love of the canned stuff. I've spent many years testing hummus recipes from the greats, soaking dried chickpeas overnight in baking soda before simmering them until perfectly tender and hand-peeling the skins from the entire batch. And that's before you even plug in the food processor. When I started hosting larger Shabbats, I wanted to offer overflowing bowls of hummus with all the fixings, but time is money, and I didn't have much of either, so I improvised.

A couple of trusty cans in my pantry began calling on me to use them like little Jewish sirens, nagging instead of singing, of course, and led me to the dark side. By using the right ratio of chickpeas to aquafaba (the starchy liquid in the can), a healthy pour of fresh lemon juice, high-quality tahini, and a heavy finger on the puree button, I whipped up a silky-smooth puree that was rich and tangy, without the faintest taste that a shortcut was used. It even swooshed perfectly! And to really bamboozle the masses, I roasted a whole head of garlic to squeeze in before blending, adding a mellowed version of sharp raw garlic with the added layer of caramelized sweetness.

If you want to spend a few days making hummus, you do you. I hear whispering positive affirmations to the chickpeas as you peel them makes your puree extra creamy. But if you're looking for the best back-pocket hummus recipe on the market, I've got you covered.

1 Preheat the oven to 400°F.

2 Rub 1 tablespoon of the olive oil over the cut sides of the garlic head, then wrap the head in aluminum foil and seal tightly. Roast the garlic for 1 hour, until caramelized and soft. Remove from the oven and let cool slightly, then squeeze out the cloves, discarding the skins.

3 Pour one can of chickpeas, liquid and all, into a food processor or high-speed blender. Drain the other can of chickpeas and add them to the food processor or blender. Add the roasted garlic, tahini, lemon juice, and a heavy pinch of salt. Puree until very smooth and creamy, 1 to 2 minutes. Taste and adjust the seasoning with salt, then transfer to a bowl. Drizzle the remaining 1 tablespoon olive oil over the hummus, then serve with pita and crudités.

Just-Add-Sour-Cream
Caramelized Onion Dip

YIELD: MAKES ABOUT 3 CUPS

PREP TIME: 15 MINUTES, PLUS
COOLING TIME

COOK TIME: 45 MINUTES

6 tablespoons (¾ stick) unsalted butter

1 pound sweet onions (about 2 medium), thinly sliced

1 pound leeks (about 2 medium), white and light green parts only, halved, rinsed well, and thinly sliced

8 sprigs thyme, tied together with butcher's twine

4 garlic cloves, thinly sliced

Kosher salt and freshly ground black pepper

½ cup minced fresh chives

2 teaspoons finely grated lemon zest

2 cups full-fat sour cream

Potato chips and crudités, for serving

While I've always loved onions, I didn't become obsessed with onion dip until Alex and I began a Sunday-night dinner tradition with his brother Avi and sister-in-law Leigh. Sometimes I'd cook huge trays of chicken parm and sometimes we'd just order an obscene amount of sushi, but every time we'd arrive to a tray of crudités with a bowl of Leigh's French onion dip, straight from the Lipton packet. The tang! The sweetness! The punch of umami! There's a reason people use it to season just about anything: the concentrated flavor of caramelized onions is simply perfect.

Onion dip was instantly absorbed into my culinary lexicon, but without the little packet. In my version, a mélange of alliums including sweet Vidalia onions, leeks, and garlic is cooked down with thyme until jammy and golden, only to be fortified with chives for more oniony goodness when cooled. To put it even simpler, you've cooked your own concentrate that simply needs a container of sour cream stirred in to be ready to go out with all the crunchy veg and potato chips you can eat!

1 In a large braiser or high-sided skillet, melt the butter over medium heat. Add the onions, leeks, thyme, garlic, and a heavy pinch each of salt and pepper. Cook, stirring often, until caramelized and jammy, about 45 minutes. Remove from the heat and let cool completely, then stir in the chives and lemon zest.

2 In a medium bowl, stir together the onion mixture and the sour cream until well incorporated. Taste and adjust the seasoning with salt and pepper, then serve with potato chips and crudités.

Note: If you're looking to prepare this recipe ahead, either make it to completion and store in an airtight container in the refrigerator for up to one day before serving, or prepare the onion mixture only and store in an airtight container in the refrigerator for up to three days before stirring with the sour cream and serving.

Roasted Eggplant and Tomato Dip
(Kashke Bademjan)

YIELD: MAKES ABOUT 4 CUPS
PREP TIME: 15 MINUTES
COOK TIME: 35 MINUTES

2 pounds eggplant (about 4 small), halved lengthwise

½ cup extra-virgin olive oil

Kosher salt

2 medium yellow onions, finely chopped

1 (6-ounce) can tomato paste

1 teaspoon ground cumin

1 teaspoon ground turmeric

¼ teaspoon cayenne pepper

3 tablespoons plain yogurt

Toasted pita or lavash, for serving

I love eggplant in any form: grilled, pureed, roasted, emoji, etc. That being said, I didn't want to throw another baba ghanoush recipe into the world. Instead, I found inspiration for this recipe from family rendezvous at kebab houses for Persian food, where plates of tomato-tinted and yogurt-drizzled *kashke bademjan* filled the table to be scooped up with warm lavash. This version involves roasting halved eggplant in the oven while you caramelize onions with tomato paste and spices on the stovetop, then blending the two together for a dip that packs some sweet heat.

In terms of serving, traditionally kashk, a fermented yogurt product, crowns the eggplant, but if I can't make it to the Persian grocery store, a swoosh of yogurt does the trick. But if you omit it, you've got a vegan dip ready to be picked up by all the carbs. Warm pita or lavash works great, as do pita chips, or even fresh crudités, if you're trying to skew healthy. In the end, dips don't lie, so give your apps all the TLC they deserve.

1 Preheat the oven to 400°F. Line a half sheet pan with aluminum foil.

2 On the prepared sheet pan, toss the eggplant with ¼ cup of the olive oil and a heavy pinch of salt to coat, then turn the halves cut-side down. Roast for 30 to 35 minutes, until tender. Let the eggplant halves cool slightly, then, using a spoon, scoop the flesh into a food processor and discard the skins.

3 While the eggplant roasts, in a large skillet, heat the remaining ¼ cup olive oil over medium heat. Add the onions and cook, stirring often, until softened and lightly caramelized, 25 to 30 minutes. Stir in the tomato paste and cook, stirring continuously, until well incorporated and caramelized to the color of rust, about 5 minutes.

Add the cumin, turmeric, and cayenne and cook, stirring, until fragrant, about 2 minutes more.

4 Transfer the onion mixture to the food processor with the eggplant and pulse until incorporated, keeping the mixture relatively chunky. Taste and adjust the seasoning with salt.

5 Transfer the dip to a bowl and top with the yogurt, swirling it gently into the dip with a spoon. Serve with toasted pita or lavash.

Note: If you're looking to prepare this recipe ahead, make it to completion with the exception of the yogurt garnish. Then, store in an airtight container in the refrigerator for up to two days before serving.

Persian Cucumber Yogurt Sauce (Mast-o-Khiar)

YIELD: MAKES ABOUT 3 CUPS
PREP TIME: 15 MINUTES

1 large English cucumber

2 cups plain full-fat Greek yogurt

½ cup chopped fresh dill

½ cup chopped fresh mint

¼ cup freshly squeezed lemon juice

Kosher salt and freshly ground black pepper

If you plan on making any kind of Persian dish, this is the side you'll need on the table. My version of this cucumber-yogurt sauce has both finely grated and minced cucumber for intense cucumber flavor with the perfect tang to spoon on your plate. Friends will ask, confused, "Isn't this tzatziki?" This is the part of the meal when I hope you shame them for trying to simplify the nuances of Levantine cuisine into one single name, given the history of Greco-Persian empires, and call out their ignorance to culinary osmosis before present-day borders were drawn!

But all that aside, this recipe is kind of a catchall. Serve it as a dip with pita chips. Toss it with shredded roasted chicken for a lighter take on chicken salad. Dollop it over any and every Persian stew. Eat it with a spoon right out of the Tupperware as you try to figure out what you want for dinner. Go crazy!

Halve the cucumber crosswise, then finely chop one half and finely grate the other. Transfer all the cucumber to a medium bowl and add the yogurt, dill, mint, and lemon juice. Stir until well incorporated. Season with salt and pepper, then serve.

Note: If you're looking to prepare this recipe ahead, make it to completion and store in an airtight container in the refrigerator for up to one day before serving.

Schmaltzy Chex Mix

YIELD: SERVES 8 TO 10
PREP TIME: 15 MINUTES
COOK TIME: 45 MINUTES

½ cup schmaltz (see page 6), melted

2 teaspoons fresh thyme leaves

1½ teaspoons kosher salt

1 teaspoon onion powder

1 teaspoon dried oregano

1 teaspoon finely grated lemon zest

1 garlic clove, finely grated

3 cups corn Chex

2 cups rice Chex

2 cups wheat Chex

2 cups Bagel Chips (page 9)

1 cup small pretzels

I'm not a huge snacker. I can restrain myself against a bag of potato chips or a bowl of popcorn, but put some Chex mix near me and I lose all control. There is just something about its combo of textures that gives me life. So, I figured I might as well throw some chicken fat on it and call it a day. I toss this snack mix with rendered schmaltz, fresh thyme, dried spices, garlic, and lemon zest before baking it low and slow until it's crisp and addictively salty/greasy.

While this munchie is perfectly good for anytime noshing, it's one of my favorite things to make the day before I host Shabbat, so I can put out a giant bowl of it when my guests arrive (it's also always better the day after you make it). It buys me a bit more time to put the finishing touches on dinner, while I enjoy my own private snack bowl.

My only disclaimer is about the pretzels. To this day, I pick out all the pretzels from store-bought Chex mix. Why? Because they are inferior to all three kinds of Chex and the mighty bagel chips used in the mix. However, I've found that gluten-free pretzels are absolutely incredible in this recipe. I don't know why, you're just going to have to trust me on this one!

1 Preheat the oven to 275°F.

2 In a small bowl, stir together the melted schmaltz, thyme, salt, onion powder, oregano, lemon zest, and garlic.

3 In a large bowl, toss the corn Chex, rice Chex, wheat Chex, bagel chips, and pretzels to combine, then drizzle with the schmaltz mixture and toss to coat. Transfer to a half sheet pan and spread into an even layer.

4 Bake, tossing halfway through, for about 45 minutes, until fragrant and crisp. Transfer to a bowl and serve warm or store in an airtight container at room temperature for up to 1 week.

Potato-Leek Bourekas

YIELD: MAKES 12 BOUREKAS

PREP TIME: 20 MINUTES, PLUS
COOLING TIME

COOK TIME: 40 MINUTES

2 tablespoons extra-virgin olive oil

1 pound russet potatoes (2 small), peeled and cut into ½-inch pieces

2 large leeks, white and light green parts only, halved, rinsed well, and thinly sliced

¾ cup whole milk

8 ounces feta cheese, crumbled

Kosher salt and freshly ground black pepper

All-purpose flour, for dusting

2 sheets store-bought puff pastry (from one 16- to 17.3-ounce package), thawed

1 large egg, beaten

White sesame seeds, for garnish (optional)

Flaky sea salt, for garnish (optional)

*B*ourekas are the Hot Pockets of the Levant, taking the flakiest of doughs and stuffing it with potatoes, spinach, meat, and/or cheese. Of all the varieties I've inhaled, potato *bourekas* may just reign supreme, wrapping creamy carbs with crispy carbs to create a portable snack that's vaguely like a Middle Eastern knish. Melted leeks are the base of my filling, adding some French vichyssoise notes when mashed with quickly simmered potatoes and tons of briny feta cheese. While you can be a hero and make everything from scratch, store-bought puff pastry totally does the trick, baking into flaky potato puffs that are fit for noshing on any time of day.

If you're looking to get even more inauthentic with your *bourekas*, I'm the guy for you. Let's say you just so happen to have leftover mashed potatoes (like my brown butter and rosemary spuds from page 11) or even mashed sweet potatoes—you can totally mix in some feta and be set with the filling. Though don't feel like you can't go the extra mile and zhuzh it up however you want with whatever is lying in your fridge. Between you and me, sometimes I throw in bacon bits, scallions, and cheddar for stuffed-potato-skin *bourekas* that would 100 percent break both the internet and my rabbi's heart.

1 Preheat the oven to 375°F. Line two half sheet pans with parchment paper.

2 In a large Dutch oven or pot, heat the oil over medium heat. Add the potatoes and leeks and cook, stirring continuously, until the leeks soften and the potatoes begin to caramelize, 5 to 6 minutes. Add the milk and stir with a wooden spoon to scrape up any browned bits on the bottom of the pot. Cover and cook until the potatoes are tender, 10 to 12 minutes. Remove from the heat and stir in the feta. Using a potato masher, coarsely mash the potato mixture, then let cool slightly. Season to taste with salt and pepper.

3 On a lightly floured cutting board, unfold 1 sheet of the thawed puff pastry (about a 9-inch square), with the seams where it was folded aligned vertically. Cut down both of the seams to make 3 strips, then cut the strips in half crosswise to form 6 equal rectangles. With your hands, take each piece and stretch it carefully into a 4-inch square.

RECIPE CONTINUES

4 Place 2 heaping tablespoons of the potato filling in the middle of each square of pastry. Brush a little beaten egg on the edges of the pastry, then fold the pastry over the filling to form triangles, stretching it as needed to enclose the filling and pinching the edges of the pastry to seal. Transfer to one of the prepared sheet pans, spacing the bourekas 2 inches apart. Repeat with the remaining sheet of puff pastry and filling to form 12 bourekas total. (You'll have a little extra filling, which can and should be saved to mix with your eggs in the morning or eaten plain with a spoon as the bourekas bake.)

5 Crimp the sealed edges of each boureka with a fork and brush each liberally with the remaining beaten egg. Sprinkle the top of each boureka with a pinch of sesame seeds and flaky sea salt, if desired.

6 Place both pans in the oven and bake, rotating the pans halfway through, for 25 to 30 minutes, until golden brown. Let cool slightly, then serve warm or at room temperature, as they're best enjoyed the same day they're baked.

Pomegranate-BBQ Chicken Wings

YIELD: SERVES 6 TO 8

PREP TIME: 30 MINUTES, PLUS 1 HOUR MARINATING TIME

COOK TIME: 55 MINUTES

FOR THE WINGS

3 pounds chicken wings, drumettes and flats separated

3 tablespoons extra-virgin olive oil

2 teaspoons kosher salt

2 teaspoons smoked paprika

1 teaspoon ground coriander

1 teaspoon garlic powder

½ teaspoon cayenne pepper

¼ teaspoon ground cloves

FOR THE POMEGRANATE BBQ SAUCE

2 tablespoons extra-virgin olive oil

2 scallions, thinly sliced

2 garlic cloves, thinly sliced

1 medium yellow onion, finely chopped

½ cup ketchup

¼ cup pomegranate molasses

¼ cup packed dark brown sugar

½ teaspoon cayenne pepper

3 tablespoons freshly squeezed lime juice

Kosher salt

Nonstick cooking spray, for greasing

Sliced scallion greens, for garnish

Pomegranate seeds, for garnish

Ground sumac, for garnish (optional)

If my childhood could be defined by one condiment, it would be KC Masterpiece BBQ sauce. My sister and I put it on anything and everything, but its primary use was for my mother's chicken wings. She'd toss the wings in a special blend of spices that had expired four years prior, then bake the wings until they were so dry, they were almost jerky, requiring a healthy squirt of our holy grail of sauces on top. The twist? They're absolutely delicious. She makes them for me to this very day, and you better believe she's still using the same expired spices.

Naturally, I had to bring my A-game if I was going to whip up an equally iconic wing recipe. Adapted for my pantry of (fresh) spices, a blend of smoked paprika, coriander, cayenne, and cloves coats the chicken, which gets oven-roasted to golden perfection. To finish, they're glazed with a sweet-and-tangy homemade BBQ sauce infused with pomegranate molasses and fresh lime juice for a kiss of Middle Eastern flavor.

Want to get ahead? You can make the BBQ sauce in advance and even toss the wings with the oil and spices to keep in the fridge for up to a day before roasting. And while I'm a boy who's all about that drumette life, you can go rogue and use this spice blend–sauce combo on non-wing cuts like drumsticks, thighs, or, dare I say it, even boneless, skinless chicken breasts. Let me become the wind beneath your wings.

1 For the wings: In a large bowl, toss the wings, olive oil, salt, paprika, coriander, garlic powder, cayenne, and cloves to coat. Cover and refrigerate for 1 hour to marinate.

2 For the pomegranate BBQ sauce: In a medium saucepan, heat the oil over medium heat. Add the scallions, garlic, and onion and cook, stirring often, until softened, 5 to 6 minutes. Stir in the ketchup, pomegranate molasses, brown sugar, and cayenne. Bring to a low simmer, then cook, stirring often, until reduced and caramelized, 8 to 10 min-

utes. Remove from the heat and stir in the lime juice. Using a blender, small food processor, or immersion blender, puree the sauce until smooth. Transfer to a bowl and season with salt.

3 Preheat the oven to 425°F. Line two half sheet pans with aluminum foil and spray the foil liberally with cooking spray.

RECIPE CONTINUES

4 Divide the wings between the pre-pared sheet pans, arranging them in a single layer. Roast, turning the wings and rotating the pans halfway through, for about 30 minutes, until lightly golden.

5 Brush the wings liberally with the BBQ sauce and return them to the oven. Roast for 10 to 15 minutes more, until caramelized and crisp.

6 Transfer the wings to a platter and garnish with sliced scallion greens, pomegranate seeds, and sumac, if desired, then serve.

Knish-Wrapped Pigs-in-a-Blanket

YIELD: SERVES 8 TO 10

PREP TIME: 30 MINUTES, PLUS 1 HOUR CHILLING TIME

COOK TIME: 25 MINUTES

3 cups (405g) all-purpose flour, plus more for dusting

1½ teaspoons baking powder

½ teaspoon kosher salt

4 ounces (1 stick) unsalted butter, melted

¼ cup vegetable oil

2 tablespoons vodka

2 tablespoons water

3 large eggs

12 all-beef hot dogs

Flaky sea salt, for garnish (optional)

Condiments of your choice, for serving

Thinking about my childhood in Queens sparks many food memories, but few are as powerful as visits to Knish Nosh. This iconic knish shop in Forest Hills was a frequent haunt for my family, where my mother would get a spread of potato knishes for me and my sister. However, our loyalty was always to the true star of the menu: the knish dough–wrapped hot dogs. With a flaky tender dough encasing a steaming, all-beef hot dog, it's the Jewish pig-in-a-blanket that I still think about constantly.

In this version, I corkscrew strips of a basic knish dough around hot dogs before baking them to golden, flaky perfection. Could you slice these into smaller sections before baking? Of course. Would you just be lying to yourself that you still wouldn't eat the equivalent of a full hot dog? Of course! Skip modesty and give the people what they deserve. To serve, you can honestly put out whatever condiments you'd like, though I personally believe mustard is the only thing that should garnish a hot dog. If you serve these with ketchup, you're dead to me!

1 In the bowl of a stand mixer fitted with the paddle attachment, pulse the flour, baking powder, and kosher salt to combine. Add the melted butter, oil, vodka, water, and 2 of the eggs. Beginning on low speed and gradually increasing to medium, mix until a smooth dough forms, about 2 minutes. Cover the dough with plastic wrap and refrigerate for 1 hour.

2 Preheat the oven to 400°F. Line a half sheet pan with parchment paper.

3 On a lightly floured work surface, roll the dough into a 16-inch square, about ¼ inch thick. Trim the edges into a clean square and cut the dough into 1-inch-wide strips. Take one of the hot dogs and wrap a strip of dough around it to cover, like a corkscrew. Place on the prepared sheet pan, then repeat with the remaining hot dogs and dough.

4 In a small bowl, beat the remaining egg until smooth. Brush the wrapped hot dogs liberally with the beaten egg and garnish each with a pinch of flaky salt, if desired.

5 Bake, rotating halfway through, for 25 to 30 minutes, until golden brown. Transfer to a platter and serve with desired condiments.

! Keeping it kosher? Swap the melted butter with margarine or vegetable oil.

Chicken Schnitzel Fingers

YIELD: SERVES 4 TO 6

PREP TIME: 35 MINUTES

COOK TIME: 15 MINUTES

2 pounds boneless, skinless chicken breasts

¾ cup plain dried bread crumbs

¾ cup panko bread crumbs

3 tablespoons white sesame seeds

3 teaspoons kosher salt

1 teaspoon garlic powder

1 teaspoon smoked paprika

1 teaspoon ground cumin

1 teaspoon cayenne pepper

¾ cup all-purpose flour

2 large eggs, beaten

Vegetable oil, for frying

Flaky sea salt

Honey mustard, for serving (optional)

As a devout lover of chicken fingers, my passion for poultry met new heights in Tel Aviv when I was introduced to Israeli schnitzel, brought to the promised land by Austrian Jews. For Israeli schnitzel, chicken—to keep things kosher, since schnitzel is traditionally made with pork—is coated in bread crumbs seasoned with Middle Eastern spices before it's pan-fried to crispy perfection. It's like regular schnitzel, but with more warmth, more love, and more flavor. Now, all I did was slice the chicken into strips to invent the schnitzel finger, but it's a truly revolutionary creation nonetheless.

To succeed at any crumb coat, it all really comes down to SBP, or standard breading procedure, the process of coating an item in the succession of flour, egg, and bread crumbs. When I worked at Daniel, there would be days when these hands breaded thousands of little saffron risotto balls, ready to be fried into golden, crispy-on-the-outside, gooey-on-the-inside canapés of bliss. Now, as a seasoned SBP veteran, I can share with you the most important piece of advice: use one hand for the dry coatings and one for the wet. By keeping the divide, you prevent your fingers from going through the same breading procedure as the chicken fingers.

1 Line a half sheet pan with parchment paper and a second half sheet pan with paper towels.

2 On a silicone cutting board, slice the chicken breasts lengthwise into 1-inch-wide strips. Using a meat mallet or the bottom of a small saucepan, pound each strip to ¼ inch thick.

3 In a shallow bowl, whisk together the bread crumbs, panko, sesame seeds, 2 teaspoons of the kosher salt, the garlic powder, paprika, cumin, and cayenne. Place the flour in another shallow bowl and the eggs in a third shallow bowl.

4 Season the chicken strips with the remaining 1 teaspoon kosher salt. Dredge each strip in the flour, shaking off any excess, then dip in the beaten egg, letting any excess drip off, and finally toss in the bread crumb mixture, pressing the crumbs against the chicken to completely coat. Arrange the breaded chickens strips on the parchment-lined pan.

5 In a large cast-iron or nonstick skillet, heat ¼ inch of oil over medium-high heat until shimmering. Working in batches, fry the chicken fingers, flipping them once, until golden brown and crisp, 2 to 3 minutes per side.

Transfer to the paper towel–lined pan to drain and immediately season with a pinch of flaky sea salt. Continue to fry the chicken, adding more oil to the pan as needed between batches (be sure to let the oil get hot before adding the next batch), until all the chicken fingers have been fried, then serve immediately with honey mustard, if desired.

Smoky Deviled Eggs

YIELD: MAKES 24 DEVILED EGGS

PREP TIME: 25 MINUTES

COOK TIME: 15 MINUTES

12 large eggs, at room temperature

⅔ cup mayonnaise

2 teaspoons white wine vinegar

1 teaspoon Dijon mustard

1 teaspoon smoked paprika, plus more for garnish

¾ teaspoon ground Urfa biber

Kosher salt

¼ cup minced fresh chives

1 celery stalk, minced

Nothing quite makes a party like deviled eggs. Hard-boiled whites filled with a silky mash of yolks, mayonnaise, and sharp mustard hit all the notes of salt, fat, and tang, all packed in a soft shell sporting a touch of minerality. If you've never had Urfa biber, let me take a moment to campaign for why it's the ingredient missing from your deviled eggs. This dried Turkish chile pepper doesn't just bring the heat, it also imparts a deep, smoky flavor to whatever you add it to. When paired with smoked paprika, the creamy combo of egg yolks and mayonnaise finds new complexity with the added veil of smoke. And if you're looking for extra kick, swap in my Horseradish Mayo (page 8)!

Everyone has their own way of cooking eggs, but this is the only way I swear by. By starting out with the water at a boil when you add the eggs, you'll have no issue easily peeling off the shell without tearing apart the white. Last but not least, don't skimp on the garnishes! When I tell you the celery and chives make the dish, I'm not kidding. They add brightness and texture at a moment when you could really use both. If you leave them off, you'll truly be the one with egg on your face.

1 Bring a large pot of water to a boil and fill a medium bowl with ice and water.

2 Using a slotted spoon, lay the eggs carefully on the bottom of the pot of boiling water. Reduce the heat to maintain a simmer and cook for 12 minutes. Using the slotted spoon, transfer the eggs to the bowl of ice water and let cool for 5 minutes, then drain.

3 Peel the eggs and slice each in half, transferring the yolks to a medium bowl and the whites to a platter, cut-side up.

4 Using a potato masher or the back of a fork, mash the egg yolks. Stir in the mayonnaise, vinegar, mustard, paprika, and Urfa biber until smooth. Season with salt.

5 Transfer the yolk mixture to a piping bag fitted with a star piping tip. Fill each egg white with about 2 tablespoons of the filling. (Alternatively, transfer the filling to a resealable plastic bag and snip off one corner to pipe, or just simply spoon the yolk mixture into the whites.)

6 Sprinkle the chives and celery over the deviled eggs, then garnish each with a pinch of paprika and serve.

Russian Nachos

YIELD: SERVES 8 TO 10

PREP: 10 MINUTES

¾ cup crème fraîche

2 teaspoons finely grated lemon zest

3 tablespoons freshly squeezed lemon juice

1 to 2 tablespoons hot water

Kosher salt and freshly ground black pepper

2 (5-ounce) bags kettle-cooked potato chips

4 ounces salmon roe

½ cup minced fresh chives

I love a good high-low combo, marrying the gourmet with the everyday pleasures that hide in your pantry. The concept of Russian nachos came from Chef Chad Brauze, a colleague and friend whom I visited when he led the kitchen of The Back Room in NYC as chef de cuisine. He brought out an amuse of freshly fried potatoes dressed with crème fraîche, herbs, and buckets of caviar, blowing my taste buds and my mind. The bridging of salty potato chips and briny caviar, wrapped up in a myriad of textures, was a combo I never stopped thinking about.

I took Chad's dish and immediately adapted it to create a version that I could serve whenever I entertain and that only takes 10 minutes to throw together. Lemon-laced crème fraîche is drizzled over bagged potato chips and topped with dollops of salmon roe and a heavy sprinkling of minced chives. It's a little bit bougie, while still being cost efficient and beyond easy to throw together. And if you're really looking to ball out, pop a bottle of champs and upgrade to some top-shelf caviar for an extra sparkle of luxury.

1 In a small bowl, whisk together the crème fraîche, lemon zest, and lemon juice until smooth. Thin out the mixture with enough hot water so it is easy to drizzle, then season with salt and pepper.

2 On a large platter, spread the potato chips into an even layer. Drizzle the lemon–crème fraîche liberally over the chips, then spoon on dollops of the salmon roe and sprinkle the chives on top. Serve immediately.

Salted Honey Chopped Liver

YIELD: SERVES 6 TO 8

PREP TIME: 15 MINUTES, PLUS 1 HOUR SOAKING TIME

COOK TIME: 25 MINUTES

1 pound chicken livers, rinsed

Kosher salt

¼ cup schmaltz (see page 6) or 4 tablespoons (½ stick) unsalted butter

2 garlic cloves, thinly sliced

1 medium yellow onion, thinly sliced

3 tablespoons honey, plus more for garnish

Flaky sea salt, for garnish

Dad jokes aside, chopped liver really is the redheaded stepchild of Jewish appetizers. To be fair, I personally think it's not as much the dish as the way it's often prepared: overcooked and underseasoned. Instead, I'm begging you to give this version a chance to change your mind, since it's inspired by the duck liver mousse served at Olmsted in Brooklyn, one of my favorite dishes in the city. Chef Greg Baxtrom saves the livers from the ducks he and his team break down and transforms them into a silky mousse, then tops it with a layer of floral honey to balance the earthy richness of the livers. It's the perfect introduction to offal cookery.

Naturally, the base of this dish is a caramelized mélange of onions and garlic cooked down in schmaltz, ready to be hit with livers you sauté until just cooked. The whole thing is then doused in honey, which caramelizes in the pan to fortify that hint of sweetness. After that, all you need is a quick chop in the food processor, and you're set. While you're gonna have to crack out the matzo for serving, try sprucing up your serving platter with bright, crunchy veg to shovel the spread into your mouth. Think fresh leaves of endive and radish quarters to add a little bite and color to this very brown recipe. Just because it's chopped liver doesn't mean it needs to be treated as such!

1 Using a paring knife, clean the livers of any visible fat or connective tissue. Transfer to a bowl with 2 heavy pinches of kosher salt and cover with cool water. Let stand at room temperature for 1 hour, then drain. Dry the livers well with paper towels.

2 In a large skillet, melt the schmaltz over medium-high heat. Add the garlic and onion and cook, stirring often, until softened and caramelized, about 15 minutes. Add the livers to the pan and season with a heavy pinch of kosher salt. Cook, stirring often, until the livers are just cooked through,

8 to 10 minutes. Stir in the honey and cook until lightly caramelized, 2 to 3 minutes. Remove from the heat and transfer to a bowl to cool slightly.

3 Transfer the liver mixture to a food processor and pulse until a coarse puree forms. Taste and adjust the seasoning with kosher salt, then transfer to a serving bowl.

4 Drizzle with more honey and finish with a pinch of flaky sea salt. Serve warm or at room temperature. This chopped liver is best served shortly after it's made.

Apples-and-Honey
Baked Brie

YIELD: SERVES 8 TO 10

PREP TIME: 20 MINUTES

COOK TIME: 30 MINUTES

8 tablespoons (1 stick) unsalted butter

2 small Honeycrisp apples, cored and thinly sliced

¼ cup honey

Kosher salt and freshly ground black pepper

6 sheets frozen phyllo dough, thawed and trimmed into 12-inch squares

1 (16-ounce) wheel Brie cheese

'm always trying to step up my apples-and-honey game. While a basic platter for dipping to sweeten the Jewish New Year is nice, I'm going more of the route of giant apples and honey cheese boards or savory-leaning tartes tatin. This baked Brie is my latest, and most popular, Rosh Hashanah creation. It's nothing fancy or complicated: simply a jumbo Brie wheel topped with sautéed apples and honey and wrapped in butter-brushed phyllo. But when baked, the combo of textures matched with the flavors of apples and honey fusing with gooey Brie never fails to please a crowd, and by crowd, I mean my family of hungry vultures.

You can keep things simple as is or add to this recipe as you please, tossing in some minced rosemary with the apples or swapping in hot honey for a little kick. You can serve slices with a fork and knife or just throw it on the table with tons of crackers and crusty bread for scooping. I'm a big believer in reducing any stress in entertaining, especially around the holidays, so please don't take your appetizers (or yourself) too seriously. Just enjoy the new year, and this new way to sweeten it!

1 Preheat the oven to 400°F. Line a half sheet pan with parchment paper.

2 In a medium skillet, heat 2 tablespoons of the butter over medium heat. Add the apples and cook, stirring often, until softened and lightly caramelized, 10 to 12 minutes. Transfer the apples to a bowl and toss with the honey. Season with salt and pepper.

3 In a small saucepan, melt the remaining 6 tablespoons butter. On the prepared sheet pan, lay out 1 sheet of the phyllo dough and lightly brush it with melted butter to coat. Lay another sheet of phyllo on top, brush with butter, and repeat this process until you've layered all 6 sheets of phyllo. Place the Brie in the center and top it with the apple mixture. Fold the corners of the phyllo sheets toward the center of the Brie, overlapping them to seal, then brush with any remaining melted butter.

4 Bake, rotating the pan halfway through, for 20 to 25 minutes, until golden brown and crisp. Transfer to a platter and serve immediately.

lots
of latkes

Hanukkah may be the festival of lights, but when it comes to the food, it's really the festival of oil. There's no better way to celebrate than with a glistening platter of freshly fried latkes begging to get smothered in applesauce and sour cream. Growing up, my mother would break out our cracked old food processor and whip up a batch. I'm not going to lie and say my mother was the best cook, but she had her specialties, and to this day, I swear she makes the best latkes on the block. (Don't @ me!) My sister and I would stand by the stove, ready to tear apart each one, shoving each piece of potato pancake immediately into ice-cold applesauce to shield our fingers from the bubbling oil.

She never had a recipe, but passed on her golden rule for golden latkes: get your hands in the mixture and give it a good ol' squeeze. Matzo meal, egg, and potato starch bind these bad boys together, but your sense of feel is most important. You're looking to just hold the shreds of potato together, since this household is not about the cakey, dense, boxed-mix version, and I will not entertain any other way! However, the longer the mixture sits, the more liquid gets pulled out of the potato and onion, which may require you to sprinkle in a little extra matzo meal to keep it all together.

While frying up a classic batch is lovely, I've developed a couple of variations that never fail to win over a crowd. The first panders to my mother's constant request for a healthier twist on, well, everything. I began using the same ratio of ingredients, but with combo of sweet potatoes and parsnips to cut out white potatoes and add just a little health

to these pan-fried treats. What I didn't expect was how much I would grow to crave this combo. The sweetness of the sweet potatoes paired with the warmth and earthiness of the parsnip creates layers of flavors you just don't expect when you bite into a latke.

The second variation came about a few years ago, when I received a text from Alex's aunt Diana recommending I add saffron to my recipe. GENIUS. I immediately broke out the box grater to give 'em a go. By adding crushed saffron to the latke mixture, not only do you get a gorgeous golden color, but each latke tastes like pieces of potato *tahdig,* marrying Ashkenazi and Mizrahi foods into a creation greater than the sum of its parts. Needless to say, these are Alex's favorite latkes ever.

As for the accouterments, I mentioned my Hanukkah table involved cold applesauce and cold applesauce only. As an adult, I swing both ways, venturing into the world of savory toppings with sour cream and all the fixings like minced chives, dill, grated fresh horseradish, salmon roe, lox, pastrami, and honestly anything else you can think of to dress up these crispy beauties. If you're feeling a little extra, like I always am, these latkes pair beautifully with my Spiced Bourbon Applesauce (page 7).

Perfect Potato Latkes

YIELD: MAKES ABOUT 10 LATKES
PREP TIME: 15 MINUTES
COOK TIME: 15 MINUTES

1 pound russet potatoes, peeled

¼ medium yellow onion

¼ cup matzo meal, plus more as needed

2 teaspoons kosher salt

2 large eggs

Vegetable oil, for frying

Applesauce, for serving

Sour cream, for serving

1 Using a box grater, coarsely grate the potatoes and onion. Transfer to a medium bowl lined with cheesecloth or a thin dish towel and wring the cloth to squeeze out any liquid into the bowl. Set the bowl of liquid aside to sit for 5 minutes. Put the squeezed potatoes and onion in another medium bowl, add the matzo meal, salt, and eggs, and mix until well incorporated.

2 Pour off and discard the reserved liquid from the first bowl, revealing a thin layer of white potato starch stuck to the bottom. Stir the potato starch into the potato mixture.

3 In a large cast-iron or nonstick skillet, heat ¼ inch of oil over medium-high heat until shimmering. Line a plate with paper towels.

4 Working in batches, scoop 3 or 4 (⅓-cup) balls of the potato mixture into the pan, spacing them 2 inches apart. Using a spatula, smash each ball to flatten. Cook the latkes, flipping once, until golden, 2 to 3 minutes per side. Transfer to the paper towel–lined plate to drain. Repeat with the remaining potato mixture, adding more oil to the pan between batches as needed (be sure to let the oil get hot before continuing with the next batch).

5 Transfer the latkes to a platter and serve immediately with applesauce and sour cream.

Root Vegetable Latkes: Swap out the russet potatoes for sweet potatoes and add 1 medium parsnip, peeled and coarsely grated, to the mix.

Saffron Latkes: Whisk the eggs with ¼ teaspoon saffron threads, finely ground with a mortar and pestle, before adding them to the potato mixture.

salads

Little Gem Salad with Pickled Celery and Tahini Dressing

YIELD: SERVES 8 TO 10

PREP TIME: 20 MINUTES, PLUS COOLING TIME

COOK TIME: 10 MINUTES

FOR THE PICKLED CELERY

1 cup white wine vinegar

⅓ cup sugar

2 tablespoons kosher salt

1 teaspoon coriander seeds

6 celery stalks, trimmed and sliced on an angle ¼ inch thick

FOR THE DRESSING

½ cup tahini

¼ cup extra-virgin olive oil

2 tablespoons freshly squeezed lemon juice

2 garlic cloves, finely grated

Kosher salt and freshly ground black pepper

FOR THE SALAD

2 pounds (6 large heads) Little Gem lettuce, trimmed and quartered

4 red radishes, thinly sliced

¾ cup toasted hazelnuts, coarsely chopped

¼ cup celery leaves (light green and yellow leaves only)

Love me a tossed salad, but for this gem of a recipe, I'll make an exception. Think of this as a modern wedge salad that packs a punch. Little Gem lettuce makes for perfect baby quarters to give that romaine-esque verdant crunch, then gets drizzled with a creamy tahini dressing and topped with toasted hazelnuts and pickled celery. Since you're already pickling the celery, which is a kind of pickle you probably didn't know you needed in your life, the brine is used to make the dressing, adding a sweet and tangy component to cut through the richness of the tahini. I encourage you to make extra dressing to keep in the fridge and use throughout the week.

Just like some of the best things in life, this salad has body to it, so it can hold up to being dressed in advanced. If you're feeling overwhelmed, feel free to assemble it completely right before your guests arrive and pop it in the fridge until you're ready to serve it. On the note of meal prep, if you make the dressing in advance and store it in the fridge, it will thicken up. Simply thin it out with a little bit of hot water until you can drizzle it, then adjust the seasoning with salt and pepper.

1 For the pickled celery: In a small saucepan, combine the vinegar, sugar, salt, coriander, and 1 cup water. Bring to a simmer over high heat and cook until the sugar and salt have dissolved, about 2 minutes. Place the celery in a heatproof bowl and pour the brine over it. Let cool completely.

2 For the dressing: In a small bowl, whisk together ½ cup of the pickled celery brine, the tahini, olive oil, lemon juice, and garlic until smooth. Season with salt and pepper.

3 For the salad: Drain the pickled celery, reserving the extra brine if desired for future batches of salad dressing. Arrange the lettuce quarters on a platter with the sliced radishes. Drizzle liberally with the dressing, then top with the pickled celery and hazelnuts. Garnish with the celery leaves, then serve.

Soy-Glazed Chicken Salad

YIELD: SERVES 4 TO 6
PREP TIME: 35 MINUTES
COOK TIME: 20 MINUTES

4 tablespoons sunflower oil or vegetable oil

1½ pounds boneless, skinless chicken breasts (3 medium)

Kosher salt and freshly ground black pepper

6 scallions, thinly sliced

4 garlic cloves, minced

1 (2-inch) piece fresh ginger, peeled and minced

¼ cup soy sauce

¼ cup rice vinegar

2 tablespoons honey

¼ teaspoon crushed red pepper

6 small mandarin oranges, 2 juiced (¼ cup juice), 4 peeled and separated into segments

1½ pounds red cabbage (1 small head), cored and thinly sliced

¾ cup salted roasted peanuts, coarsely chopped

1 head iceberg lettuce, cored and thinly sliced

¾ cup sesame sticks

There's something about an Asian-inspired chicken salad that just makes me go wild! It's a healthyish salad that's filling enough to be a full meal, and it sparks vivid memories of my mother ordering it at any restaurant that served it. This version takes all those flavors and converts them into a big-ass dinner salad that's become my go-to for low-lift entertaining and weeknight meal prep. Soy-glazed chicken is tossed with iceberg lettuce (my favorite lettuce of all time), red cabbage, mandarin orange segments, peanuts, and sesame sticks to cover pretty much every texture and flavor you'd want in a salad. Is it authentic? Hell, no. Delicious? You betcha!

Honestly, what sets this salad apart from any other recipe you'll find is the dressing. Instead of throwing out the schmaltzy pan drippings, full of soy, honey, caramelized garlic, ginger, and scallions, I just whisk in some fresh mandarin orange juice and more oil and call it a day. You already put in the work to build up all that flavor, so I want to make sure you get to enjoy every last drop. Any leftovers of the dressed salad will hold up beautifully in the fridge for a day. The only warning I have is about the sesame sticks, which serve as the almighty croutons in this recipe—if they're added to the salad ahead of time, they'll turn into soggy mush. Keep them as a final garnish to ensure they add the glorious crunch they're intended to.

1 Preheat the oven to 350°F.

2 In an ovenproof medium skillet, heat 2 tablespoons of the oil over medium-high heat. Season the chicken with a heavy pinch each of salt and black pepper. Sear the chicken, flipping once, until golden, 5 to 6 minutes per side. Transfer to a plate.

3 Reduce the heat to medium. Add the scallions, garlic, and ginger to the skillet and cook until fragrant, about 1 minute. Stir in the soy sauce, vinegar, honey, and crushed red pepper. Return

the chicken to the pan, turning it to coat. Transfer the skillet to the oven and roast for 8 to 10 minutes, until the chicken reaches an internal temperature of 165°F. Remove from the oven and transfer the chicken breasts to a cutting board. Let rest for 10 minutes, then cube.

4 Transfer any pan juices from the skillet to a small bowl and whisk in the remaining 2 tablespoons oil and the orange juice. Season with salt and black pepper.

5 In a large bowl, toss the cubed chicken, orange segments, cabbage, peanuts, and lettuce with the dressing until well coated. Taste and adjust the seasoning with salt and black pepper. Top with the sesame sticks and serve immediately.

Challah Panzanella

YIELD: SERVES 6 TO 8

PREP TIME: 30 MINUTES

COOK TIME: 15 MINUTES

1 (16-ounce) loaf challah bread (page xvii), cut into 2-inch cubes

½ cup balsamic vinegar

½ cup extra-virgin olive oil

2 tablespoons minced fresh oregano

1 medium red onion, thinly sliced

Kosher salt and freshly ground black pepper

2 pounds heirloom tomatoes, cored and cut into 1-inch chunks

1 pound Persian cucumbers (6 medium), halved lengthwise and cut into 1-inch-thick pieces

1 pound fresh mozzarella, cut into ½-inch cubes

1 cup packed fresh basil leaves, roughly torn

In yet another effort to use up day-old Shabbos challah (see Rose Water and Cardamom French Toast, page 29, and Challah Croque Monsieur, page 39), this panzanella salad was born, marrying all the sunny flavors of the warmer months with my love for eating lots of bread and calling it "salad." Toasted challah cubes become sponges for the bright juices of tomatoes tossed with balsamic-marinated onions, cukes, and fresh oregano. Naturally, I throw in a pound of mozzarella just for the hell of it, giving the people what they want, wrapped up in all those summer caprese vibes.

For peak enjoyment, toss the salad right before serving, since you want the outside of the croutons soft and saturated in the dressing while keeping the centers crisp. Feel free to make the marinated onions a day ahead, but that's about all the advance prep I'd recommend without compromising the integrity of this summer superstar.

1 Preheat the oven to 375°F.

2 Spread the challah pieces in an even layer over a half sheet pan. Bake for 15 to 20 minutes, until dry and crisp. Remove from the oven and let cool.

3 Meanwhile, in a large bowl, stir together the vinegar, olive oil, oregano, and onion to combine. Season with a heavy pinch each of salt and pepper, then let sit at room temperature for 15 minutes to marinate.

4 Add the tomatoes, cucumbers, mozzarella, and basil to the bowl with the marinated onion and toss to coat. Gently fold in the challah croutons. Taste and adjust the seasoning with salt and pepper, then serve.

Tomato-Cucumber Salad (Salad-e Shirazi)

YIELD: SERVES 6 TO 8

PREP TIME: 20 MINUTES

2 pounds Persian cucumbers (12 medium), diced

½ cup chopped fresh parsley leaves and tender stems

½ cup chopped fresh mint

2 pounds vine-ripe tomatoes (6 medium), cored and chopped

1 medium red onion, diced

¼ cup freshly squeezed lemon juice

¼ cup extra-virgin olive oil

Kosher salt

Tomato-cucumber salad sure can cause a ton of conflict, depending on what you call it. Food definitely is political, but for today, we're just going to keep it as light as, well, this salad. I started making this dish, named after the city of Shiraz in Iran, to accompany the Persian feasts I would prepare for Alex. It offers a bright crunch to offset the often heavy bowl of rich stew over buttery rice, and is as simple as can be. Given its prevalence across the Middle East and Mediterranean, it can pair with pretty much any dish from either culinary canon.

With a little precision, you can prep this dish in advance so it takes almost no effort to get it onto the table. In one container, I store the chopped cucumbers and herbs; in another, the chopped tomatoes and onion; and in a third one, the lemon juice and olive oil. This prep can be done up to a day in advance, and the salad tossed together with salt just before your guests arrive. The salt will begin to pull out the juices from the vegetables, which combine with the lemon juice and oil to form a flavorful dressing that coats the salad. Fair warning: Toss it too far in advance, and you'll end up with a dish closer to gazpacho than salad!

In a large bowl, toss the cucumbers, parsley, mint, tomatoes, onion, lemon juice, and olive oil to combine. Season with salt, then let sit for 10 minutes. Toss again to distribute the dressing, then serve immediately.

Kale Tabbouleh Salad

YIELD: SERVES 8 TO 10

PREP TIME: 25 MINUTES, PLUS 1 HOUR SOAKING TIME

COOK TIME: 20 MINUTES

1½ cups cracked bulgur wheat

3 cups warm water

2½ pounds butternut squash (1 large), peeled, seeded, and cut into 1-inch pieces

½ cup plus 2 tablespoons extra-virgin olive oil

Kosher salt and freshly ground black pepper

½ cup freshly squeezed lemon juice

3 garlic cloves, finely grated

2 pounds lacinato kale, leaves stemmed and thinly sliced

1 cup fresh parsley leaves and tender stems, coarsely chopped

½ cup hulled pumpkin seeds (pepitas), toasted

2 Honeycrisp apples, cored and coarsely chopped

This salad is dedicated to Lynn Schusterman! Lynn is not just my hero, but also an iconic philanthropist and cofounder of the Charles and Lynn Schusterman Family Foundation, which supports some incredible organizations I've been involved with like OneTable, Jewish Food Society, and REALITY Israel. To put it simply, I don't know a better person. I had the privilege of going on REALITY Israel, a Schusterman initiative that gathers leaders in different industries and sends them on a weeklong trip to Israel. I was one of fifty individuals—spanning chefs, food writers, spirits-makers, farmers, and everything in between—on the food-focused "Taste" trip. There, I became close with the very talented James Beard award–winning chef Zach Engel of Galit, in Chicago, who probably doesn't know how much I was fangirling when I met him. While we rubbed mud on each other at the Dead Sea and spoon-fed one another labneh ice cream overlooking Tel Aviv, this salad is truly what bonds us the most.

Zach made this dish for me when he was visiting New York, and I was shook. I thought I knew kale salad, but as is the case with most things, I knew nothing. Tossed in a garlic-and-lemon dressing, shreds of kale were layered with chewy bulgur, crisp Honeycrisp apples, chunks of nutritional yeast–crusted delicata squash, and *baharat*-spiced pepitas for probably the best salad I've ever had. It had every flavor. It had every texture. It was balanced and delicate and hearty and I think about it often . . . more often than anyone should be thinking about salad. So much so that I started making my own simpler adaptation, bumping up the bulgur for some heft, swapping in a simply roasted butternut squash for the delicata, and throwing in a little parsley for a classic touch to this very inauthentic take on tabbouleh. I'm no Zach, or Lynn, but a boy can dream!

1 Preheat the oven to 450°F.

2 Put the bulgur in a large bowl and add the warm water. Let stand for 1 hour, then drain off any excess water.

3 Meanwhile, on a sheet pan, toss the butternut squash with 2 tablespoons of the olive oil and a heavy pinch each of salt and pepper. Roast, tossing once halfway through, for 16 to 18 minutes, until tender. Switch the oven to broil and broil for 3 to 4 minutes, until the squash is nicely charred.

4 In a large bowl, whisk together the remaining ½ cup olive oil, the lemon juice, and the garlic. Season with salt and pepper. Add the kale and parsley to the bowl and toss with the dressing, massaging the greens gently with your hands (but don't get crazy—it's just salad).

5 Add the bulgur, roasted squash, pepitas, and apples to the bowl with the greens and toss to combine. Taste and adjust the seasoning with salt and pepper, then serve.

yom kippur break-fast

Atoning for your sins by fasting on Yom Kippur really builds up an appetite, so bring on the bagels! Don't skimp on the lox—you're worth it.

———

vegetables

Date-Roasted Brussels Sprouts

YIELD: SERVES 4 TO 6
PREP TIME: 20 MINUTES
COOK TIME: 20 MINUTES

2 pounds Brussels sprouts, trimmed and halved

3 tablespoons coconut oil, melted

½ teaspoon crushed red pepper

Kosher salt

3 tablespoons date syrup (silan)

5 Deglet Noor dates, pitted and coarsely chopped

There's something about adding a little sugar to vegetables that just gives me life. Maybe it's the way the veg ends up caramelizing in the oven for a crispy, golden exterior; maybe it's the way the flavors begin to sing; or maybe it's just because I use so much salt that a little sweetness gives my palate a reprieve. Either way, date syrup has become one of my favorite pantry staples for next-level vegetable cookery.

While I'm very into drizzling it over my morning yogurt (especially with a handful of Persian-ish Granola, page 40), using date syrup to give a little caramelization boost to veggies has become a roasting tip I can't help but scream from the rooftops. Call me crazy, but the combo of chopped dates and date syrup actually gives me bacon vibes. The salt, sugar, and spice with the crispy texture of the date chunks makes for some excitement with your sprouts that has had my family requesting them at every feast I prepare.

Honestly, tweaked for timing, this recipe would work with winter squashes or any root vegetables you have on hand. The secret is adding both forms of dates in the final 10 minutes of high-temp roasting so they don't burn! If you're really in a pinch, maple syrup is a great substitute for date syrup, but do yourself a favor and order a few bottles. You're worth it.

1 Preheat the oven to 450°F.

2 On a half sheet pan, toss together the sprouts, melted coconut oil, crushed red pepper, and a heavy pinch of salt to coat, then spread into an even layer on the pan.

3 Roast the sprouts for 12 minutes, then remove from the oven and toss with the date syrup and chopped dates. Return the pan to the oven and roast for 10 to 12 minutes more, until the sprouts are caramelized and tender. Taste and adjust the seasoning with salt, then serve.

Citrusy Cumin-Roasted Carrots

YIELD: SERVES 6 TO 8

PREP TIME: 10 MINUTES

COOK TIME: 30 MINUTES

2 pounds small rainbow carrots, scrubbed

3 tablespoons extra-virgin olive oil

1 tablespoon cumin seeds

¼ teaspoon crushed red pepper

Grated zest and juice of 1 navel orange

Kosher salt

My mother always used to make carrots for every holiday meal. She'd throw baby carrots in a large bowl with some water and microwave them until tender. *Et voilà!* While we will not shame her because she's still an icon, it definitely was not her most iconic dish. However, it didn't stop those baby carrots from causing a screaming-and-crying fight between her and my aunt one Passover seder long ago. The power root vegetables have!

Family drama aside, while working at ABC Kitchen in NYC years back under Chef Dan Kluger, I was introduced to what happens when you treat carrots like the star of the show. ABC Kitchen's iconic roasted carrot salad took days to make, and honestly, trying that salad felt like the first time I'd truly tasted the vegetable. While I'm not about to have you spend three days making a side dish, this particular recipe is a minor revelation. Whole cumin seeds perfume the pan, while fresh orange juice steams the carrots before reducing down into a glaze to highlight their natural sweetness. I'll often assemble it the day before to marinate in a reusable resealable bag so I just need to throw the carrots on a sheet pan to roast before serving.

Please note that a key part of this recipe is carrot girth. Obviously, girth is lovely for so many of life's pleasures, but not here. If you end up with jumbo carrots (wider than ¾ inch), halve them lengthwise so they cook through evenly. If you happen to get carrots with the tops attached, don't throw out those greens! Rinse them well, since they may be sandy, and throw them in the blender with some olive oil, garlic, lemon juice, and salt for a bright puree to drizzle over the finished platter.

1 Preheat the oven to 450°F.

2 On a half sheet pan, toss together the carrots, olive oil, cumin, crushed red pepper, orange zest, orange juice, and a heavy pinch of salt to coat, then spread into an even layer on the pan. Roast the carrots for 30 to 35 minutes, until golden and tender. Taste and adjust the seasoning with salt, then serve.

Roasted Cauliflower with Pistachios and Golden Raisins

YIELD: SERVES 6 TO 8

PREP TIME: 15 MINUTES

COOK TIME: 30 MINUTES

½ cup plus 3 tablespoons extra-virgin olive oil

1 tablespoon ground coriander

1 tablespoon freshly ground black pepper

Kosher salt

2 medium heads cauliflower (2½ pounds), leaves intact, each head cut into 6 wedges

¼ cup raw pistachios, coarsely chopped

¼ cup golden raisins

¼ teaspoon ground cardamom

¼ cup chopped fresh parsley leaves and tender stems

Cauliflower will always be a vegetable near and dear to my heart. After Alex and I signed our ketubah, the Jewish marriage certificate, we took our families to Eyal Shani's Miznon in New York's Chelsea Market, where we had a huge spread of pitas and a dozen of their famous whole roasted cauliflower. Golden on the outside, with the creamiest interior, it's my muse every time I buy a head of cauliflower to cook. Instead of florets, I break each head down into six thick wedges for optimal surface area to get brown and delicious. (Those trendy cauliflower steaks fall apart and are stupid, so we'll be cooking chunky wedges in this house.) On top, cardamom-scented raisins and pistachios add the perfect sweetness and texture to tie the whole dish together (you may want to make a little extra for a chef snack). It's a side dish that may just outshine any main on your table!

When it comes to roasted cauliflower, I have a few pearls of wisdom to offer. First, add some water to the pan. The water steams the wedges in the oven, then evaporates to let them get golden and crisp. Second, if you don't get the color you want by the time the stems are tender, throw on the broiler for a few minutes! And last but not least, don't trim the stem and leaves. They're my favorite parts of the whole cauliflower, so don't let them end up in the trash!

1 Preheat the oven to 450°F.

2 In a small bowl, stir together ½ cup of the olive oil, the coriander, pepper, and a heavy pinch of salt. Spread the cauliflower wedges in a single layer over a half sheet pan and rub them with the olive oil mixture. Pour ⅓ cup water into the pan, then roast the cauliflower for 30 to 35 minutes, until golden and tender. (If you still need more color, switch the oven to broil and broil the cauliflower for 2 to 3 minutes.)

3 Meanwhile, in a small saucepan, combine the remaining 3 tablespoons olive oil, the pistachios, raisins, and cardamom. Cook over medium heat until the pistachios are toasted and the spices are fragrant, 3 to 4 minutes. Transfer to a bowl and stir in the parsley, then season with salt.

4 Transfer the roasted cauliflower to a platter and spoon over the pistachio mixture, then serve.

Za'atar-Roasted Eggplant with Tahini

YIELD: SERVES 4 TO 6

PREP TIME: 15 MINUTES

COOK TIME: 35 MINUTES

2 pounds Italian eggplant (4 small), halved lengthwise

⅓ cup extra-virgin olive oil

2 tablespoons za'atar

1 teaspoon finely grated lemon zest

Kosher salt and freshly ground black pepper

⅓ cup tahini

2 tablespoons freshly squeezed lemon juice

1 garlic clove, finely grated

¼ cup warm water

2 tablespoons date syrup (silan)

Fresh mint leaves, for garnish

Pomegranate seeds, for garnish

Flaky sea salt, for garnish

I cook a whole lot of eggplant in this book because it's one of the most versatile veggies, and can take on a myriad of textures depending on how you cook it. This roasted number is a meatier vegetable side that can stand up to any protein, or even stand in for one as the topper for your next grain bowl. Halved eggplant is roasted in a lemony za'atar oil to take on an herbaceous tang before getting drizzled with garlicky tahini for richness and date syrup for a sweet finish. It tastes like you put in a lot more effort than you actually did, which is the ultimate sign of a great dish!

If you take away anything from this recipe, it's the love of a crosshatch. For any ingredient like eggplant that soaks up flavor, scoring the flesh allows the flavors to penetrate deeper, while creating more surface area for crispy edges. The key is using a sharp knife and a delicate hand, since you don't want to cut all the way through to the skin of the eggplant. As for the eggplant itself, this may be the only time in life where a small eggplant is preferred. I find the jumbo ones to be tough in texture and packed with too many seeds, so try for a modest 8-ouncer. And in the summer, try this recipe with the tiny Fairy Tale eggplants you'll find at the farmers' market—they're my favorite!

1 Preheat the oven to 425°F. Line a half sheet pan with parchment paper.

2 Score the flesh of each eggplant half with a paring knife, making a series of ½-inch-long slices (about ¼ inch deep) on the diagonal and then another round of slices perpendicular to the first, creating a crosshatch pattern. Place the eggplant cut-side up on the prepared sheet pan.

3 In a small bowl, whisk together the olive oil, za'atar, lemon zest, and a heavy pinch each of kosher salt and pepper. Pour the mixture over the eggplant, rubbing it into the crosshatches.

4 Roast the eggplant for 35 to 40 minutes, until tender when pierced with a paring knife.

5 Meanwhile, in a small bowl, whisk together the tahini, lemon juice, garlic, and warm water until smooth. Season with kosher salt and pepper.

6 Transfer the eggplant to a platter and drizzle with the tahini sauce and date syrup. Garnish with the mint leaves, pomegranate seeds, and a pinch of flaky sea salt, then serve.

Baharat Smashed Potatoes

YIELD: SERVES 4

PREP TIME: 15 MINUTES

COOK TIME: 45 MINUTES

2 pounds multicolor baby potatoes, scrubbed

Kosher salt

⅓ cup extra-virgin olive oil

1 teaspoon freshly ground black pepper

1 teaspoon ground sumac

1 teaspoon ground coriander

1 teaspoon ground cumin

½ teaspoon ground cinnamon

¼ teaspoon ground allspice

¼ teaspoon ground cardamom

Schug (Green Yemeni Hot Sauce, page 11), for serving

Plain and simple, smashed potatoes are the best potatoes. Combining the best aspects of all preparations, you boil baby potatoes for the creaminess of a baked potato, but then smash them to jack up the surface area before roasting, resulting in a level of crispiness even a french fry could not achieve. This is the only recipe that never seems to yield any leftovers, no matter how much extra I make. I personally think the magic is all in the seasoning.

This mixture is my super-simplified recipe for *baharat*, an essential Arabic spice blend integral in Iraqi Jewish cooking, which combines warm spices like allspice and cardamom with sharper spices like black pepper and cumin. Every family truly has their own blend, so it's not uncommon to find fennel seeds, rosebuds, nutmeg, chiles, or a laundry list of other aromatics present as well. It's becoming more and more common to find jars of premixed *baharat* at specialty spice shops, so feel free to sub 1½ tablespoons of your favorite *baharat* blend in lieu of the spices called for here.

To finish off these crunchy spiced potatoes, a drizzle of *schug* on the finished platter helps provide the zip that makes this dish truly irresistible.

1 Preheat the oven to 450°F.

2 Put the potatoes in a large pot and add cold water to cover by 2 inches. Season the water with 2 heavy pinches of salt. Bring to a simmer over medium-high heat, then cook the potatoes until tender when pierced with a fork, 12 to 15 minutes. Drain, running the potatoes under cold water until they are cool enough to handle.

3 Using the bottom of a measuring cup or glass, smash each potato on a cutting board until ¼ inch thick. Transfer to a half sheet pan, spreading the potatoes out in an even layer.

4 In a small bowl, whisk together the olive oil, pepper, sumac, coriander, cumin, cinnamon, allspice, cardamom, and a heavy pinch of salt. Drizzle the spiced oil over the smashed potatoes and gently toss to coat.

5 Roast the potatoes, flipping them once halfway through, for 30 to 35 minutes, until golden brown and crisp. Taste and adjust the seasoning with salt.

6 Transfer the potatoes to a platter, drizzle with schug, and serve.

Spicy Herb-Roasted Mushrooms

YIELD: SERVES 2 TO 4

PREP TIME: 10 MINUTES, PLUS 15 MINUTES STEEPING TIME

COOK TIME: 35 MINUTES

¼ cup extra-virgin olive oil

3 garlic cloves, thinly sliced

1 fresh serrano chile, stemmed and thinly sliced

2 sprigs thyme

Zest of 1 lemon, peeled with a vegetable peeler

1 pound mixed fresh mushrooms, such as maitake, oyster, and king trumpet, roughly torn

Kosher salt

When Alex and I got married at Sunday in Brooklyn, one of our favorite New York restaurants, we had two conditions for the menu: 1) That they serve their life-changing pastrami cod for the dinner, since it might be the best fish option to ever grace a wedding feast; and 2) that they serve their wood-fired maitakes, since it's 100 percent the best mushroom dish on the planet. I'm talking crispy edges and chewy centers for concentrated bites of umami that can stand up on their own to any protein.

As someone who grew up thinking they hated mushrooms, this dish sent me down the rabbit hole of perfecting mushroom cookery so I could convert those like me who wrote off fungi too early. I've learned that 'shroomies are little sponges for fat and flavor, so what better way to inject the vibrance of herbs, chiles, and garlic than infusing it in the dish's cooking oil for a punch of flavor.

While you could use sliced portobellos or quartered creminis here, I'm begging you to explore the fancy section at the store (or maybe even make a special trip to the farmers' market). Maitake, oyster, and king trumpet mushrooms have become absolute favorites of mine for their flavor and texture when roasted, though I love that you could honestly use a pound of whatever you can get your hands on for this recipe. As for the potent oil tincture, it could also be used for anything from roasting other veggies to making salad dressings to stirring into pasta for a little kick. Hell, put out a bowl of it and dip in some bread!

1 Preheat the oven to 450°F.

2 In a small saucepan, combine the olive oil, garlic, and serrano. Cook over medium-low heat until the edges of the garlic begin to turn golden, 4 to 5 minutes. Remove from the heat and gently add the thyme and lemon zest (the oil will pop a little). Let steep for 15 minutes, then strain the oil through a fine-mesh sieve into a bowl and discard the solids.

3 On a half sheet pan, toss the mushrooms with the infused oil and a heavy pinch of salt. Roast the mushrooms, tossing once halfway through, for 30 to 35 minutes, until golden and crisp. Taste and adjust the seasoning with salt, then serve.

Brown Butter–Rosemary Mashed Potatoes

YIELD: SERVES 8 TO 10
PREP TIME: 25 MINUTES
COOK TIME: 30 MINUTES

2¾ pounds russet potatoes (5 medium), peeled and cut into 1-inch pieces

Kosher salt

8 ounces (2 sticks) unsalted butter

2 cups heavy cream

3 sprigs rosemary

Freshly ground black pepper

These mashed potatoes make me feel like I'm wearing oversize sweatpants while cuddling under a gravity blanket. It's a giant, starchy, buttery hug that I want you to make for any occasion where there is a roast chicken or brisket present. While I totally get the kosher restrictions, I've always been baffled why more secular Jews don't serve their brisket over mashed potatoes. Gravy? Yea, it's fine. But brisket sauce?! Now *that's* what I want to be smothering my two-sticks-of-butter bowl of taters with.

Not to get too science-y, but I'm Team Russet when it comes to my mash, since they're high in starch and low in moisture, resulting in a velvety texture when mashed. As for the process, I'd recommend investing in a potato ricer (it looks like a giant version of your mother's garlic press) to achieve a super-smooth consistency. If you only have a handheld masher, that will work, too—I'm not one to ever shame chunky mashed potatoes.

For those who are looking to keep things on the lighter side, turn the page! There's no world in which I wouldn't recommend doing the absolute most with your mashed potatoes by adding brown butter and rosemary-infused cream. My Shabbat practice is all about gratitude, so you better believe I'm grateful to be able to manage my cholesterol. It's all about portion control, anyway, so treat yourself.

1 Put the potatoes in a large pot and add cold water to cover by 2 inches. Season the water with 2 heavy pinches of salt. Bring to a simmer over medium-high heat, then cook the potatoes until tender when pierced with a fork, 15 to 18 minutes. Drain.

2 Meanwhile, in a medium saucepan, melt the butter over medium-high heat. Cook, stirring continuously, until browned and nutty in aroma, 6 to 8 minutes. Slowly stir in the cream and rosemary, then reduce the heat to medium and bring to a light simmer. Cook until fragrant and infused, about 5 minutes. Using a slotted spoon, remove the rosemary and discard. Season with a heavy pinch each of salt and pepper, then keep warm.

3 Pass the cooked potatoes through a potato ricer or food mill back into the pot. Stir in the cream mixture until incorporated and smooth. Taste and adjust the seasoning with salt and pepper, then serve.

Sautéed Asparagus with Apricot and Lemon

YIELD: SERVES 4
PREP TIME: 15 MINUTES
COOK TIME: 15 MINUTES

2 tablespoons extra-virgin olive oil

1 pound asparagus, ends trimmed

Kosher salt and freshly ground black pepper

2 tablespoons apricot preserves

2 tablespoons freshly squeezed lemon juice

¼ teaspoon crushed red pepper

Truly, there is some kind of fascination with Jewish families and serving sad, limp asparagus at the High Holidays. It typically comes down to convenience: a bunch of asparagus tossed with a little bit of oil and an even more minuscule amount of salt. That being said, I love asparagus for entertaining. It's simultaneously delicate in flavor and hearty in texture! It cooks quickly! It makes your pee smell funny!

This recipe gives the most respect to every stalk with a tag-team cooking method of sautéing and steaming. This allows them to get a bit of caramelization and color before they're steamed until tender, while keeping that vibrant green color intact. To finish, apricot preserves and lemon add a touch of sweetness and tang to this stellar side dish.

1 In a large skillet, heat the olive oil over medium-high heat. Add the asparagus and cook, tossing often, until lightly golden, 5 to 6 minutes. Season with a heavy pinch each of salt and black pepper.

2 Add the apricot preserves, lemon juice, crushed red pepper, and 2 tablespoons water to the pan. Cover the pan with the lid ajar and steam until most of the liquid has evaporated and the asparagus are tender, about 2 minutes. Taste and adjust the seasoning with salt and black pepper, then serve.

Pickle Juice–Braised Cabbage

YIELD: SERVES 6 TO 8

PREP TIME: 15 MINUTES

COOK TIME: 25 MINUTES

⅓ cup extra-virgin olive oil

3 garlic cloves, thinly sliced

¼ teaspoon crushed red pepper

3 pounds red cabbage (1 large), cored and thinly sliced

1½ cups half-sour pickle juice (from a jar of pickles)

1 tablespoon sugar

Kosher salt and freshly ground black pepper

½ cup chopped fresh dill

Cabbage is hands-down one of the most underrated vegetables. You can ferment it. You can stuff it. You can turn it into coleslaw! And most important, you can braise it to make one of the easiest side dishes ever. I've made no new discoveries here with this age-old cooking technique. I have vivid memories of leaving class in culinary school with my chef's coat stained with a splatter of purple polka dots and radiating the pungent odor of cabbage. And honestly, I wasn't mad. I adore its toothsome texture and the vibrant color picked up from the addition of vinegar or lemon juice. Hell, I don't even mind being perfumed with a little eau de sauerkraut. But then I discovered using leftover pickle juice as the braising liquid, and that's when things really got interesting.

To shed light on this epiphany, we first need to address that my mother is a fridge hoarder. Much to my chagrin, she refuses to throw out anything in her little icebox, and please don't get me started on her freezer. One day, I was braising some cabbage in her apartment, as any nice Jewish boy would, when I stumbled upon a jar of pickle juice sitting in the fridge, without a single pickle inside. (Her excuse was that she slices up fresh cucumbers to add to the leftover brine for a little half-sour action, but the jury's still out on that one.) I made the executive decision to use the juice for the braised cabbage and found the silver lining in my mother's questionable refrigerator habits: this recipe. Pickle juice adds the perfect acidity to tinge the whole pot a vibrant fuchsia, while imparting complexity with its hint of fermented funk. My mother loved it so much, the Tupperware of leftovers received the coveted spot on the top shelf of the fridge, balanced over the almost-empty jar of pickle juice—the highest honor!

1 In a large pot or Dutch oven, heat the olive oil over medium heat. Add the garlic and cook, stirring, until lightly golden and fragrant, 2 minutes.

2 Add the crushed red pepper, immediately followed by the cabbage. Cook, stirring often, until the cabbage begins to wilt, 5 to 7 minutes.

3 Stir in the pickle juice and season with the sugar and a heavy pinch each of salt and black pepper. Cover and cook until the cabbage is tender and a vibrant purple, about 15 minutes. Remove from the heat and stir in the dill. Taste and adjust the seasoning with salt and black pepper, then serve.

carbs

Fancy Mushroom Kasha Varnishkes

YIELD: SERVES 4 TO 6
PREP TIME: 15 MINUTES
COOK TIME: 40 MINUTES

Kosher salt

4 ounces (1 stick) unsalted butter

1 pound mixed fresh mushrooms (such as maitake, oyster, or beech), roughly torn

2 medium yellow onions, finely chopped

Freshly ground black pepper

1 cup kasha (toasted whole buckwheat groats)

3 cups chicken stock or vegetable stock

16 ounces dried farfalle (bow-tie) pasta

½ cup chopped fresh parsley leaves and tender stems

½ cup chopped fresh dill

Grated zest and juice of 1 lemon

I discovered this Ashkenazi side in New York's Murray Hill neighborhood when my husband and I would make our weekly visit to Sarge's Delicatessen for a bowl of matzo ball soup. Made with kasha (cooked buckwheat groats) and bow-tie pasta and flavored with caramelized onions and tons of butter, *kasha varnishkes* tastes like a big bowl of pasta had a Jewish lovechild with a grain bowl. I became obsessed with the chewy texture of whole buckwheat groats and started stocking my pantry with the Eastern European staple (you can find it in many supermarkets and it's easily available online). To liven things up, I transformed the side dish into a weeknight pasta that I serve as the main attraction more often than not.

While you may think the secret to this recipe is that I throw in tons of mushrooms and onions caramelized in butter, which definitely doesn't hurt, but the real magic is simmering the kasha in chicken stock. I keep things brothy so the buckwheat is tender before it has absorbed all the liquid. This allows the al dente pasta to suck up the rest of the stock as it finishes cooking, adding more flavor while also coating the noodles in a glossy sauce. Finished with lemon and herbs to brighten up this rich pot of carbs, it's the flashiest *kasha varnishkes* you'll ever make.

1 Bring a large pot of salted water to a boil. Cover and keep at a gentle bubble until you are ready to cook the pasta.

2 In a medium Dutch oven or pot, melt the butter over medium heat. Add the mushrooms, onions, and a heavy pinch each of salt and pepper. Cook, stirring occasionally, until the mushrooms and onions are softened and caramelized, 20 to 25 minutes. Transfer to a bowl.

3 Add the kasha to the Dutch oven and cook, stirring continuously, until lightly toasted, about 2 minutes. Add the stock and a heavy pinch each of salt and pepper. Cover and cook until the kasha is tender but has not absorbed all the liquid, about 10 minutes.

4 Meanwhile, bring the pot of water back to a boil and add the pasta. Cook, stirring occasionally, until al dente, 9 to 10 minutes, then drain.

5 Add the mushroom mixture and the pasta to the pot with the buckwheat. Cook for 2 minutes to incorporate the flavors.

6 Remove from the heat and stir in the parsley, dill, and lemon zest and juice. Stir until well combined, then taste and adjust the seasoning with salt and pepper. Let stand for 2 minutes to soak up any remaining liquid, then give everything one last toss and serve.

Fresh Za'atar Pesto Risotto

YIELD: SERVES 6 TO 8

PREP TIME: 20 MINUTES

COOK TIME: 30 MINUTES

My love language is carbs. And luckily, it's my husband's, too. I learned early on in our relationship that flowers will never be able to compete with whipping up a big pot of starchy risotto to surprise him when he gets home from work. It's a perfectly simple dish with few ingredients, but you can taste the constant care and attention that's needed to make it properly. To keep things fresh in our relationship, I'm always switching up the mix-ins, creating an endless list of risotto possibilities. This Middle Eastern spin began with the crazy idea to create a pesto that incorporated the same flavors as za'atar, combining fresh oregano, tangy sumac, toasted sesame seeds, Parmesan, and tons of olive oil. I swirled it into the creamy, mascarpone-spiked rice and never looked back.

Given how easy the pesto is to make, let's make sure you're giving the rice the love it deserves. The velvety texture of risotto comes from the constant agitation of short-grain rice, which releases starch into the cooking liquid to thicken it into a glossy sauce. That means you can't step away from the pot, even for a min-ute, and you'll want to add the liquid slowly to ensure you shake the most starch out of your rice. This is why you have to bring the stock to a simmer in a separate pot. If it's not bubbling away, the stock will take drastically longer to get absorbed into the rice, and nobody has time for a two-hour risotto. Finally, if you can't tell when your rice is ready, pull out a grain and press it down on your counter with your finger, revealing smaller white dots of starch. If you see three visible dots, your risotto is not done cooking. However, once you see two specks, you're ready to party!

And if you become as obsessed with this za'atar pesto as I am, don't let risotto be the only excuse to blend up a batch. Toss it with cooked pasta to serve either hot for a dinner party or cold for a summer pasta salad. Drizzle it over fresh heirloom tomatoes and mozzarella for a Middle Eastern caprese salad. Mix it with mayo and discover the condiment you never knew you needed for schmearing on sandwiches and dipping fries into.

FOR THE ZA'ATAR PESTO

2 cups packed fresh parsley leaves and tender stems

½ cup packed fresh oregano leaves

¾ cup extra-virgin olive oil

½ cup freshly grated Parmesan cheese, plus more for garnish

2 teaspoons finely grated lemon zest

¼ cup freshly squeezed lemon juice

¼ cup pine nuts, toasted (see tip)

2 tablespoons white sesame seeds, toasted (see tip)

2 teaspoons ground sumac

1½ teaspoons kosher salt

2 garlic cloves

FOR THE RISOTTO

8 cups chicken stock or vegetable stock

Kosher salt and freshly ground black pepper

2 tablespoons unsalted butter

½ medium yellow onion, minced

2 cups Arborio rice

½ cup white wine

¼ cup mascarpone cheese

1 For the pesto: In a blender, combine the parsley, oregano, olive oil, Parmesan, lemon zest, lemon juice, pine nuts, sesame seeds, sumac, salt, garlic, and ¼ cup water. Blend until smooth.

2 For the risotto: In a medium saucepan, bring the stock to a light simmer. Season with a heavy pinch each of salt and pepper.

3 In a medium Dutch oven or pot, melt the butter over medium heat. Add the onion and cook, stirring often, until softened, 4 to 6 minutes. Add the rice and cook, stirring continuously, until lightly toasted and fragrant, about 2 minutes.

4 Add the wine and cook, stirring continuously, until it has been completely absorbed, 1 to 2 minutes. Using a ladle, add about 1½ cups of the simmering stock to the rice. Cook, stirring continuously, until the liquid has been completely absorbed. Continue this process of adding the stock in increments and stirring until you have used up all the stock and the rice is tender, 20 to 25 minutes total.

5 Remove the risotto from the heat and stir in the pesto and mascarpone until incorporated. Taste and adjust the seasoning with salt and pepper. Divide among serving bowls and garnish with Parmesan, then serve.

❗ Hot and Toasty Nuts Whenever I'm working with nuts, seeds, or whole spices, I like to toast them first to awaken their oils, so they'll add more flavor to whatever they touch. Simply throw them in a skillet and toast over medium heat, stirring continuously, until fragrant and lightly golden, 3 to 5 minutes. Alternatively, you can toast them in the oven, a method I love for larger nuts like cashews or pistachios. Arrange them in a single layer on a rimmed sheet pan and bake in a preheated 350°F oven for 5 to 10 minutes, until fragrant and lightly golden. Note that in a recipe where the nuts, seeds, or whole spices will end up going into the oven—like the pistachios and pine nuts in my Persian-ish Granola (page 40), the sesame seeds for garnishing my challah recipe, and the cumin seeds in my Citrusy Cumin-Roasted Carrots (page 98)—you shouldn't toast them in advance or you'll risk the chances of them burning.

One-Pot Persian-ish Pasta

YIELD: SERVES 4 TO 6
PREP TIME: 15 MINUTES
COOK TIME: 25 MINUTES

3 tablespoons extra-virgin olive oil

1 medium yellow onion, thinly sliced

1 teaspoon ground turmeric

16 ounces dried linguine

1 (15-ounce) can chickpeas, drained and rinsed

1 (15-ounce) can red kidney beans, drained and rinsed

Kosher salt and freshly ground black pepper

5 ounces baby spinach

½ cup chopped fresh cilantro leaves and tender stems

½ cup chopped fresh mint

Laziness just comes naturally to me. As much as I love pouring my heart and soul into a Shabbos feast, I equally adore pouring a bunch of random things in one pot and calling it a night. This one-pot pasta is inspired by one of my favorite Persian soups, *ash-e reshteh,* which is a vegetarian stunner of slow-cooked beans with turmeric-stained onions, linguine-like noodles, and chopped fresh herbs that slowly turn army green as they melt into the broth.

I first tried the soup at break-fast with Alex's aunt Diana, a self-proclaimed lazy cook, who ladled out bowls from the slow cooker she now makes the dish in. In typical Jewish fashion, she apologized in advance for the soup not being as good as it usually is, though it was honestly magical. The starch from the beans and noodles added body to the broth, while the chopped greens added a freshness that cannot be matched. I feel warm and cozy just writing about it.

Not that it's a competition, but this extremely loose version of *ash-e reshteh* is even lazier, since I've taken the element of low-and-slow cooking out of the equation. Instead, this recipe combines all the main flavors and cooks them down into a luscious, creamy pasta that's ready in less than 30 minutes. It's the furthest thing from authentic (hence the generic name), but it's still my go-to for a hearty weeknight meal!

1 In a large high-sided skillet or braiser, heat the olive oil over medium-high heat. Add the onion and cook, stirring often, until softened and lightly caramelized, 8 to 10 minutes. Stir in the turmeric and cook until fragrant, about 1 minute.

2 Pour in 5½ cups water, then add the linguine, chickpeas, kidney beans, and a heavy pinch each of salt and pepper. Bring to a simmer and cook, stirring often, until the pasta is al dente and the liquid has reduced to a creamy sauce, about 15 minutes.

3 Stir in the spinach, cilantro, and mint and cook until wilted, about 2 minutes. Remove from the heat. Taste and adjust the seasoning with salt and pepper, then serve.

Cardamom–Spiced Pear Noodle Kugel

koo-koo
for kugel

Spinach–Artichoke Kugel

I love noodle kugel, and I'm not ashamed of it. It's a dairy-packed dish that doesn't know if it's a side or a dessert, offering a custardy bread pudding–like center with crispy edges of curly egg noodles and pockets of plump raisins. As a kid, how couldn't you love an excuse to eat dessert with dinner, only to get a second round after? As an adult, the tables have turned. If I'm cooking a meal, I want every dish to work together, and somehow the thought of brisket and sweet noodle kugel on the same plate just makes me gag. So welcome to my whimsical world of modern kugel, where I break all the rules to get my peers hyped about Jewish casseroles.

To start, don't be afraid to go savory. With a base of cottage cheese, sour cream, and eggs, kugel can venture in whatever direction you want, so let's go wild and make it pasta-party strong enough to stand on its own. Toss in mounds of grated Gruyère and cheddar for a Jewish mac and cheese that my husband accurately describes as *dank*.

Getting ready for game day? I'm certainly not, but that doesn't mean I can't celebrate my love for spinach-artichoke dip by throwing all the same components in with the egg noodles. I give you permission to think of savory kugel as a garbage can casserole, a way to give new life to all your leftovers, from roasted veggies and random meats to wilting herbs and cheeses that have seen better days.

Now, if you're like me and still crave the nostalgic sweet noodle kugel, know that you are seen! I've fallen head over heels for the combo of brown butter, cardamom, and pears, which offers warmth and richness and allows you to go light on the sugar. It's the gateway casserole to lure any sweet kugel–averse loved one over to the dark side. I've had it for dinner. I've had it for dessert. I've had it for breakfast in my underwear straight out of the fridge. There are no wrong answers.

Strapped for time? The best part of this kugel triumvirate is that any can be assembled and baked a few hours in advance, then set aside until you're ready to serve—all you'll have to do is reheat, which is one less thing to worry about when entertaining. That being said, if you've got the bandwidth, flaunt it, and bake your kugel right before serving. Thank you in advance for supporting my cause of making kugel cool again!

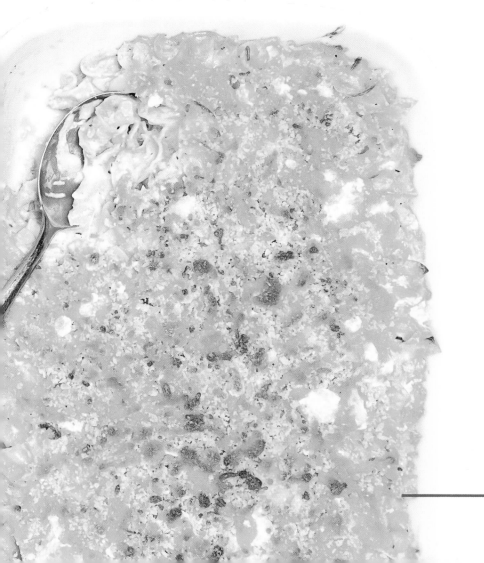

Kugel and Cheese

Kugel and Cheese

YIELD: SERVES 10 TO 12

PREP TIME: 20 MINUTES

COOK TIME: 35 MINUTES

Kosher salt

1 pound sharp cheddar cheese, coarsely grated

8 ounces Gruyère cheese, coarsely grated

8 ounces fresh mozzarella, coarsely grated

2 cups full-fat cottage cheese

1 cup full-fat sour cream

2 teaspoons chopped fresh rosemary

1 teaspoon chopped fresh thyme

¼ teaspoon freshly grated nutmeg

4 large eggs

12 ounces dried wide egg noodles

1 cup panko bread crumbs

2 tablespoons extra-virgin olive oil

1 Preheat the oven to 375°F. Bring a large pot of salted water to a boil.

2 In a medium bowl, toss the cheddar, Gruyère, and mozzarella to combine.

3 In a blender, combine the cottage cheese, sour cream, rosemary, thyme, nutmeg, 2 teaspoons salt, and eggs. Blend until smooth.

4 Add the egg noodles to the boiling water and cook until al dente, 4 to 5 minutes, then drain and transfer to a large bowl.

5 Add the egg mixture and two-thirds of the grated cheeses to the bowl with the noodles and toss to combine. Pour the mixture into a 9 by 13-inch baking dish and spread it into an even layer.

6 Add the panko to the bowl with the remaining grated cheeses and toss to combine. Sprinkle the panko mixture over the noodles and drizzle with the olive oil.

7 Bake for 30 to 35 minutes, until the kugel is golden brown and set. Serve immediately.

Spinach-Artichoke Kugel

YIELD: SERVES 10 TO 12

PREP TIME: 30 MINUTES

COOK TIME: 1 HOUR

Kosher salt

2 cups full-fat cottage cheese

1 cup full-fat sour cream

1 cup packed fresh parsley leaves and tender stems

1 cup freshly grated Parmesan cheese

6 large eggs

4 ounces (1 stick) unsalted butter

1 medium yellow onion, thinly sliced

2 garlic cloves, thinly sliced

1 pound frozen artichoke hearts, thawed and coarsely chopped

1 pound baby spinach

½ teaspoon crushed red pepper

12 ounces dried wide egg noodles

1 Preheat the oven to 375°F. Bring a large pot of salted water to a boil.

2 In a blender, combine the cottage cheese, sour cream, parsley, ½ cup of the Parmesan, 2 teaspoons salt, and eggs. Blend until smooth.

3 In a large Dutch oven, melt the butter over medium heat. Add the onion and garlic and cook, stirring often, until softened and lightly caramelized, 12 to 15 minutes. Add the artichoke hearts, spinach, and crushed red pepper, then cook, stirring continuously, until the artichokes are warmed through and the spinach has wilted, 4 to 5 minutes. Remove from the heat and season with salt.

4 Add the egg noodles to the boiling water and cook until al dente, 4 to 5 minutes, then drain and transfer to a large bowl.

5 Add the egg mixture and the spinach-artichoke mixture to the bowl with the noodles and toss to combine. Pour the mixture into a 9 by 13-inch baking dish and spread it into an even layer. Sprinkle the remaining ½ cup Parmesan evenly over the top.

6 Bake for 40 to 45 minutes, until the kugel is golden brown and set. Remove from the oven and let cool for 10 minutes, then serve warm.

Cardamom-Spiced Pear Noodle Kugel

YIELD: SERVES 10 TO 12
PREP TIME: 20 MINUTES
COOK TIME: 50 MINUTES

Kosher salt

4 ounces (1 stick) unsalted butter

2 cups full-fat cottage cheese

1 cup full-fat sour cream

¼ cup packed light brown sugar

1 teaspoon ground cardamom

6 large eggs

12 ounces dried wide egg noodles

4 medium Anjou pears, cored and coarsely chopped

1 Preheat the oven to 375°F. Bring a large pot of salted water to a boil.

2 In a medium saucepan, melt the butter over medium-high heat. Cook, stirring continuously, until browned and nutty in aroma, 6 to 8 minutes. Transfer to a heatproof bowl and let cool slightly.

3 Pour the brown butter into a blender and add the cottage cheese, sour cream, brown sugar, 2 teaspoons salt, cardamom, and eggs. Blend until smooth.

4 Add the egg noodles to the boiling water and cook until al dente, 4 to 5 minutes, then drain and transfer to a large bowl.

5 Add the egg mixture and the pears to the bowl with the noodles and toss to combine. Pour the mixture into a 9 by 13-inch baking dish and spread it into an even layer.

6 Bake for 40 to 45 minutes, until the kugel is golden brown and set. Remove from the oven and let cool for 10 minutes, then serve warm.

Robina's Polo with Tahdig (Crispy Persian Rice)

YIELD: SERVES 6 TO 8
PREP TIME: 20 MINUTES, PLUS 1 HOUR SOAKING TIME
COOK TIME: 40 MINUTES

In almost every food culture, there's an obsession with the "crispy bits." Whether it's the crunchy pieces of pasta at the corners of a lasagna or the coveted edge pieces clinging to the side of the brownie pan, we'd fight friends and family to the death for these prized morsels. Perched on this pedestal in Persian cuisine, *tahdig* may be the best crispy bit of them all. Literally translating to "bottom of the pot," it's the crispy layer that forms when rice is cooked low and slow. When you invert the pot onto a platter to serve, a mound of fluffy saffron rice is crowned with the golden, crisp *tahdig,* holding everything together until you break it open like a piñata. It's just what you need to soak up any Persian stew or kebab. I do not know a better rice!

A few months into dating my husband, I arrived home to find a package from his mother. It contained two gifts that—as I've since discovered—every Persian mother sends to her child's significant other: a Persian rice cooker and a copy of *Food of Life,* the Iranian cooking bible by Najmieh Batmanglij. The package was a not-so-subtle signal: learn how to make Alex's favorite Persian dishes or else she would start shipping frozen Tupperwares of stews to keep him well-fed. I didn't need much convincing, since, much as I had with Alex, I fell head over heels in love with Persian cuisine, and especially with *tahdig.*

My mother-in-law, Robina, taught me her method, which to this day is what my recipe is based on. She parboils long-grain basmati rice and then tosses part of it with a rich mixture of yogurt, saffron water, and tons of oil (though I use exclusively butter, of course). The inclusion of yogurt—a trick borrowed from *tahchin,* a heavenly baked Persian rice casserole often stuffed with chicken—helps the crust stay together and cook evenly. And while not every family uses yogurt in their *tahdig,* I find it makes the dish so much more luxurious! That yogurt-coated mixture lines her rice cooker before getting topped with the remaining rice and a lot more saffron water and oil. With the press of a button, the rice cooker goes to work, spitting out a perfectly golden *tahdig* every time.

Call me a glutton for punishment, but I was set on learning how to make it in a pot the old-fashioned way. I persevered through many failed attempts, involving both burnt and soggy rice, in order to get to where I am today. After mastering the classic dish, I eventually added many nontraditional variations to my repertoire, like latke *tahdig* and buffalo chicken *tahchin* (see pages 134 and 135).

Before we get too far, let's go over some tips to help novices venturing into the magnificent realm of crispy Persian rice come out in one piece.

First things first: Invest in a cheap nonstick skillet. To this day, I use a pot I saved from Alex's bachelor apartment kitchen, and I swear by it! I'm not going to add any science to this piece of advice—just trust me. Once you've got your vessel, practice makes perfect. The terrifying thing about this dish is your inability to see how it's cooking until you flip it out. You need to birdbox the situation, so familiarize yourself with the smells and sounds the rice makes. Listen for a gentle, slow sizzle, which tells you the rice is slowly getting golden and not scorching, and then smell for a toasty aroma to know when it's ready. You'll also want to wrap the pot lid in a kitchen towel before you cover the pot to absorb steam and prevent the crust from getting soggy.

To be honest, my heart still drops a little each time I flip a *tahdig* out of the pot, but this recipe has never steered me wrong!

3 cups uncooked basmati rice, rinsed

3 tablespoons kosher salt

¼ teaspoon saffron threads, finely ground with a mortar and pestle

¼ cup boiling water

8 tablespoons (1 stick) unsalted butter, melted

½ cup plain full-fat Greek yogurt

1 large egg yolk

1 Put the rice in a large bowl and add cold water to cover by 1 inch and 1 tablespoon of the salt. Let soak for 1 hour, then drain.

2 Meanwhile, in a medium bowl, combine the saffron with the boiling water, then let sit until bright red, about 10 minutes. Whisk in 1 tablespoon of the salt and 6 tablespoons of the melted butter.

3 In another medium bowl, whisk the yogurt and egg yolk with half the saffron butter until smooth.

4 Bring a large pot of water to a boil. Season with the remaining 1 tablespoon salt. Add the rice and boil until just tender but not fully cooked, about 5 minutes, then drain.

5 Grease a shallow 10-inch nonstick pot with the remaining 2 tablespoons melted butter. Gently stir 3 cups of the parboiled rice into the yogurt mixture until the rice is well coated. Spread the coated rice over the bottom of the greased pot and 2 inches up the sides. Top with the remaining parboiled rice, then drizzle the remaining saffron butter over the top.

6 Wrap a kitchen towel around the lid of the pot, covering the bottom, then place the lid on the pot. Place the pot over medium-high heat and cook until you begin to hear the rice sizzling loudly, 4 to 5 minutes. Reduce the heat to low and cook until the rice is golden brown, 20 to 25 minutes. To know when the tahdig is ready, you'll begin to smell toasted rice and you can even take a peek at the side with a spatula to ensure the edges are golden.

7 Remove from the heat and run a rubber spatula around the sides of the pot to ensure the rice doesn't stick. Place a platter over the pot and carefully but quickly invert them together, remove the pot so the crispy rice is on top, then serve.

Tahchin: Paralyzed with fear? You'll still get a flawless crust if you lean in further to tahchin, the baked Persian casserole the yogurt mixture from the crust is borrowed from. Assemble it (or the sweet potato, latke, and other variations that follow) in a greased 9-by-13-inch glass baking dish, then cover tightly with aluminum foil and bake at 400°F for about 2 hours. The best part is you can see the bottom to ensure it's golden before flipping it out of the dish.

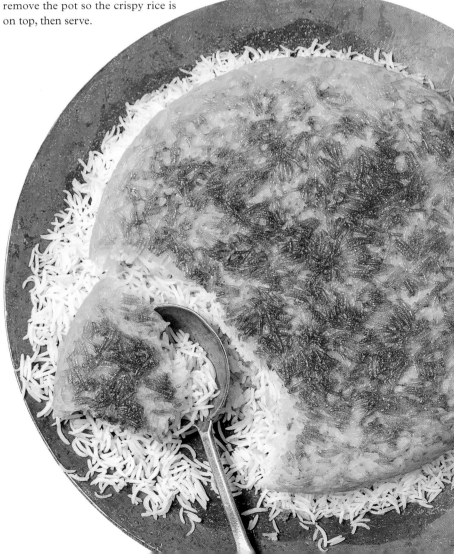

Want to skip the dairy? Swap the butter for vegetable oil and either swap the yogurt for a plain unsweetened nondairy yogurt (I like coconut the best) or omit it altogether. If you want it vegan, leave out the egg yolk, too.

Potato Tahdig: Peel 1 small russet potato and slice it ¼ inch thick, then toss it with 1 tablespoon of the saffron water. Place the slices over the bottom of the greased pot before layering the yogurt-coated rice on top, making sure the rice fills any holes between slices of potato. Continue with the recipe as written.

Sweet Potato Tahdig: Peel 1 small sweet potato and slice it ¼ inch thick, then toss it with 1 tablespoon of the saffron water. Place the slices over the bottom of the greased pot before layering the yogurt-coated rice on top, making sure the rice fills the holes between slices of sweet potato. Continue with the recipe as written.

Buffalo Chicken Tahchin: Press the yogurt-coated rice over the bottom of a greased 9-by-13-inch glass baking dish, covering it completely. In a large bowl, toss 3 cups shredded rotisserie chicken, ½ cup plain full-fat Greek yogurt, 4 tablespoons (½ stick) melted butter, and ¼ cup hot sauce to combine. Season with salt, then layer the chicken evenly over the rice. Top with the remaining parboiled rice, drizzle with the remaining saffron-butter mixture, and cover tightly with aluminum foil. Bake at 400°F for about 2 hours. Check the bottom to ensure it's golden before flipping it out of the dish.

Pasta Tahdig: Omit the rice and ignore steps 1 and 4. Cook 16 ounces dried bucatini until al dente, then toss the cooked noodles with the yogurt mixture. Using tongs or your hands, drape strands of the noodles around the bottom of the pot to make a swirl design. Top with the remaining pasta, drizzle with the remaining saffron-butter mixture, and continue with the recipe as written.

Latke Tahdig: Make my Saffron Latkes (page 78) and press the uncooked latke mixture over the bottom of the greased pot. Continue with the recipe as written.

soups
+ stews

Saffron Chicken Noodle Soup

YIELD: SERVES 8 TO 10

PREP TIME: 20 MINUTES

COOK TIME: 1 HOUR 45 MINUTES

FOR THE BROTH

1 (3- to 4-pound) whole chicken

8 cups chicken stock

½ teaspoon saffron threads, finely ground with a mortar and pestle

1 medium yellow onion, halved crosswise

1 carrot, halved crosswise

1 celery stalk, halved crosswise

2 sprigs thyme

1 dried bay leaf

Kosher salt and freshly ground black pepper

FOR THE SOUP

3 medium carrots, diced

3 celery stalks, diced

2 medium parsnips, peeled and diced

6 ounces dried medium egg noodles

¼ cup minced fresh parsley leaves and tender stems

¼ cup minced fresh dill

1 teaspoon finely grated lemon zest

Kosher salt and freshly ground black pepper

There's a good reason they call chicken soup Jewish penicillin: it literally cures everything. Whenever Alex is sick, I always whip up a giant pot of chicken noodle soup. And if we're both sick, my mother makes the delivery. That being said, this recipe is just as good for cold-weather entertaining as it is for reviving sickly bodies. Memories of my mother chopping bunches of curly parsley and dill fill my head every time I crave a bowl. There would be herbs sprinkled all over the kitchen by the time she was done, as she insisted on using a tiny serrated knife to chop them, but the soup still came out absolutely perfect every time!

I'd love to give an elaborate inspiration for the addition of saffron, but honestly, I was playing nurse and just threw some from the pantry into the mix. I was blown away by how a little bit infused the broth so beautifully for an upgrade in flavor and color. After slowly simmering the chicken and veggies to fortify your golden broth, fresh veggies, herbs, and egg noodles build up a hearty mélange. Your bubbe could never!

1 For the broth: In a large pot, combine the whole chicken, stock, saffron, onion, carrot, celery, thyme, bay leaf, and 6 cups water. Bring to a simmer over medium-high heat, then reduce the heat to maintain a low simmer and cook until the chicken is tender and the broth has reduced by a third, about 1 hour 30 minutes.

2 Transfer the chicken to a bowl and let cool slightly, then strain the broth into a large bowl, discarding all the solids. Season the broth with salt and pepper.

3 When the chicken is cool enough the handle, use two forks to shred the meat and discard the skin and bones. Set the meat aside.

4 For the soup: Return the strained broth to the pot and bring to a simmer over medium-high heat. Add the carrots, celery, and parsnips and cook, reducing the heat as needed to maintain a simmer, until tender, 10 to 12 minutes. Add the shredded chicken and the egg noodles and cook until the noodles are al dente and the chicken is heated through, 5 to 6 minutes. Remove from the heat and stir in the parsley, dill, and lemon zest. Taste and adjust the seasoning with salt and pepper, then ladle the soup into bowls and serve.

Iraqi Beet Kubbeh Soup
(Kubbeh Shawandar Hamudh)

YIELD: SERVES 8 TO 10
PREP TIME: 2 HOURS, PLUS 1 HOUR
30 MINUTES RESTING AND CHILLING TIME
COOK TIME: 1 HOUR AND 10 MINUTES

I take immense pride in having brought matzo ball soup and its magical Ashkenazi healing properties into Alex's life, but he was quick to return the favor. Not long into dating, Alex introduced me to *kubbeh*, a dish originating from Iraqi and Kurdish Jewish communities, offering an equally spiritual soup experience. *Kubbeh* are meat-stuffed dumplings that can be cooked in an array of broths, from delicate and floral to hearty and earthy. (Technically *kubbeh* can also be fried and served without soup, but let's save that lesson for another time!) In the Iraqi Jewish community, one of the most popular preparations of *kubbeh* involves the sweet-and-sour beet broth you see here, which tinges the *kubbeh* with the prettiest shade of fluorescent crimson-red. It's a Mizrahi masterpiece!

My initial goal as I embarked on my *kubbeh* apprenticeship was to perfect the recipe as Alex knew it. After all, just as every region has its variation of *kubbeh*, so does every family. All I had to do was consult with Alex's aunties—the keepers of the family's largely untranscribed food traditions. Simple, right? Wrong. While I had hoped that interviews with Alex's matriarchs would steer me on a clear path, what I discovered instead was a conflicting set of instructions that made it difficult to determine *which* variation of *kubbeh* to represent.

In my first attempt to learn the dish, I chased Auntie Lilian around her kitchen with a scale and measuring cups in hopes of transcribing her recipe. Lilian grinds her own rice and chicken for her dough and then stuffs her dumplings with chopped chicken. It was delicious, but Alex insisted I also take a note from Auntie Majdolin, who uses beef for her filling, which he prefers. Then, of course, I made *kubbeh* for my mother-in-law, Robina, who informed me that her mother never used ground rice for her dough, but used semolina instead.

So began my experiments, wherein I rolled hundreds of *kubbeh* to test every possible variable and variation. After each test, I summoned Alex and Robina into the kitchen to taste, and I eagerly awaited their feedback. "*La b'dalek*," Robina would tell me. The Judeo-Iraqi Arabic equivalent of "No, darling," would always precede her list of thoughtful critiques. Slowly but surely, my batches did keep getting better, until one day, I was given their blessings on the version you find here. (Cue the clip of Valerie Cherish screaming, "Well, I got it!")

And while it was a blast to get lost in the scientific meticulousness of recipe testing, what brings me the most joy is that this is now the first written-down recipe of *kubbeh* in Alex's family, preserving a most delicious part of his family's culinary tradition.

FOR THE KUBBEH DOUGH

8 ounces (1 medium) chicken breast, roughly chopped

2 cups coarse semolina

2 teaspoons kosher salt

FOR THE KUBBEH FILLING

1 pound ground chicken or lean ground beef

½ medium yellow onion, minced

½ cup minced fresh parsley leaves and tender stems

2 teaspoons kosher salt

1 teaspoon ground turmeric

½ teaspoon freshly ground black pepper

FOR THE BROTH

3 pounds red beets with stems and leaves (6 medium)

¼ cup extra-virgin olive oil

1 medium yellow onion, minced

2 teaspoons ground cumin

2 teaspoons ground coriander

1 teaspoon sweet paprika

1 teaspoon ground turmeric

¼ teaspoon cayenne pepper

3 garlic cloves, minced

¼ cup tomato paste

½ cup freshly squeezed lemon juice

3 tablespoons sugar, plus more as needed

2 tablespoon kosher salt, plus more as needed

¼ cup minced fresh parsley leaves and tender stems

Rice, for serving

1 For the dough: In a food processor, combine the chicken with ¼ cup water and process until a smooth paste forms, scraping as needed.

2 Transfer to a large bowl with the semolina, salt, and ½ cup water. Using your hands, mix together to make a smooth dough. Cover with plastic wrap and let sit at room temperature for 45 minutes.

3 For the filling: Meanwhile, in a medium bowl, mix together the chicken or beef, onion, parsley, salt, turmeric, and pepper until well combined.

4 To assemble the kubbeh, line a half sheet pan with parchment paper and set a small bowl of water nearby. Using wet hands, press 1 tablespoon of the dough mixture in the palm of your hand into a thin 2½-inch round. Spoon 1 tablespoon of the filling into the center, then carefully fold over the dough to seal and roll it into a smooth ball. Place it on the prepared sheet pan, then continue until all the dough and filling have been used (you should have about 45 kubbeh). Freeze the kubbeh, uncovered, for 45 minutes.

5 For the broth: Meanwhile, remove the stems and leaves from the beets and wash them thoroughly. Rip the leaves from the stems; coarsely chop the leaves, then thinly slice the stems, reserving both separately. Peel the beets and slice each into 12 wedges.

6 In a large pot, heat the olive oil over medium-high heat. Add the onion and cook, stirring often, until softened and lightly caramelized, 5 to 6 minutes. Stir in the cumin, coriander, paprika, turmeric, cayenne, and garlic and cook, stirring, until fragrant, about 1 minute. Stir in the tomato paste and cook, stirring continuously, until lightly caramelized, 2 to 3 minutes.

7 While stirring, slowly add 10 cups water to the pot, followed by the beet wedges, lemon juice, sugar, and salt. Bring to a simmer over medium high heat, then cover, reducing the heat to maintain a simmer, and cook until the beets are tender, 30 to 35 minutes.

8 Stir the chopped beet stems into the broth, then gently add the kubbeh. Return the broth to a simmer, cover, and cook until the kubbeh are cooked through and tender, about 30 minutes. Remove from the heat and stir in the beet greens and parsley. Taste and adjust the seasoning with sugar and salt, then serve over rice. (It's always better the next day!)

Short Rib Cholent

YIELD: SERVES 8 TO 10

PREP TIME: 20 MINUTES

COOK TIME: 2 HOURS 55 MINUTES

3 tablespoons vegetable oil

Kosher salt and freshly ground black pepper

3 pounds medium bone-in short ribs, patted dry

1 yellow onion, thinly sliced

2 garlic cloves, smashed and peeled

2 tablespoons honey

2 teaspoons smoked paprika

8 cups beef stock

1½ pounds red potatoes (4 medium), scrubbed and quartered

1 cup dried navy beans, soaked overnight and drained (see tip, page 151)

1 cup uncooked pearled barley

½ cup chopped fresh parsley leaves and tender stems

¼ cup chopped fresh chives

I'm going to take a bit of poetic license and say that *cholent* is kind of like a Jewish mash-up of baked beans and beef-barley soup. Truth be told, I had never even heard of this dish until I began writing about Jewish food. Let's have a little storytime to understand why it may be foreign to many Reform Jews like myself!

We begin in the shtetls of Eastern Europe, where Jews needed to find a way to serve hot food on Saturday, without having to light a fire or cook on the Sabbath. Women would bring clay pots of assembled but uncooked stews to the local baker to throw in the oven, since it would remain hot enough to cook them through the night. The next day, the pots would be picked up, ready to serve after temple. Families would throw in whatever scraps of meat they had, stretching the stews with barley, beans, and potatoes to make a meal hearty enough to fill them up until sunset.

Now that we have some context, it's time to make this nontraditional version of *cholent,* which adapts many of the classic components into a one-pot braised short rib recipe that's sure to stun. While I'm all about this low-and-slow braise in the oven, I won't be mad if you adapt this recipe for your slow cooker, as long as you don't skip searing the short ribs first. It's a little sweet, a little smoky, and extremely hearty. It's shtetl chic!

1 Preheat the oven to 325°F.

2 In a large Dutch oven, heat the oil over medium-high heat. Season the short ribs with 2 heavy pinches each of salt and pepper. Working in two batches, sear the short ribs, turning them as needed, until golden brown, 8 to 10 minutes per batch. Transfer the seared ribs to a platter.

3 Add the onion and garlic to the pot and cook, stirring often, until softened and lightly caramelized, 4 to 5 minutes. Stir in the honey and paprika and cook until fragrant and the honey is lightly caramelized, 1 to 2 minutes.

4 Pour in the stock, scraping up any browned bits on the bottom of the with a wooden spoon, then return the short ribs to the pot. Stir in the potatoes, beans, and barley. Season with 2 heavy pinches each of salt and pepper and bring to a simmer. Cover the pot and transfer it to the oven. Braise for 2 hours 30 minutes to 3 hours, until the beans and barley are cooked and the short ribs are extremely tender.

5 Serve the short ribs whole, or remove them from the pot, discard the bones, and coarsely chop the meat, then return it to the pot. Gently stir in the parsley and chives, then taste and adjust the seasoning with salt and pepper. Divide the cholent among serving bowls and serve.

Roasted Chicken
Matzo Ball Soup

YIELD: SERVES 6 TO 8

PREP TIME: 30 MINUTES, PLUS 1 HOUR CHILLING TIME

COOK TIME: 1 HOUR

How do you like your balls? It's one of the more divisive questions in the Jewish community. Obviously, I'm referring to balls of the matzo variety, but I'm happy to discuss all others in my DMs. The two schools of thought we shall debate today are small and dense or huge and fluffy. As you know, for every five Jews there about fifteen opinions, but this happens to be a topic that I don't passionately take a side on. My balls fall somewhere in between, greased up with a healthy amount of schmaltz. I want them to be fluffy and easily scooped with the touch of a spoon, while also modest in size, so I can have two, of course.

You can easily make these matzo balls and add them to my Saffron Chicken Noodle Soup (page 138), but I wanted to create a flavorful broth that was easy to throw together, since if you're making matzo balls, you're probably cooking up a storm for entertaining, a holiday, or both. By roasting the chicken legs and vegetables first, you're able to fortify the golden broth faster while imparting even more flavor. And you better believe I have chunks of chicken and vegetables in my broth. There's nothing sadder than matzo balls served in chicken soup without any of the chicken, so I'm giving you all the meat you deserve.

My only request: If you make this recipe, be sure to send me a pic of your balls!

RECIPE CONTINUES

2 cups matzo meal

½ cup schmaltz (see page 6), melted

2 tablespoons minced fresh dill

2 teaspoons kosher salt, plus more as needed

6 large eggs, beaten

⅔ cup seltzer water

FOR THE SOUP

2 pounds bone-in, skin-on chicken legs (4 medium)

1 pound carrots (4 medium), scrubbed and cut into 1-inch pieces

1 pound parsnips (4 large), scrubbed and cut into 1-inch pieces

1 medium yellow onion, diced

2 tablespoons extra-virgin olive oil

Kosher salt and freshly ground black pepper

8 cups chicken stock

¼ cup minced fresh dill

1 teaspoon finely grated lemon zest

1 For the matzo balls: In a large bowl, stir together the matzo meal, melted schmaltz, dill, salt, and eggs until smooth. Gently stir in the seltzer until incorporated. Cover and refrigerate for 1 hour.

2 Bring a large pot of salted water to a boil. Scoop the chilled matzo mixture into ¼-cup balls, using wet hands to roll them until smooth. You should have about 14 matzo balls. Gently add the matzo balls, one at a time, to the boiling water. Reduce the heat to maintain a simmer, cover, and cook until fluffy and tender, about 1 hour. Remove from the heat, cover, and let sit for 15 minutes, then keep warm until the soup is ready.

3 For the soup: While the matzo balls cook, preheat the oven to 450°F.

4 On a half sheet pan, toss together the chicken legs, carrots, parsnips, onion, olive oil, and a heavy pinch each of salt and pepper, then arrange the legs skin-side up on the pan. Roast for 30 minutes, until the vegetables and chicken are lightly golden.

5 Transfer the vegetables and chicken to a large pot and cover with the stock and 4 cups water. Bring to a simmer over medium-high heat, then reduce the heat to maintain a low simmer and cook until the chicken is extremely tender, about 30 minutes. Using a ladle, skim off any fat from the top of the liquid and discard. Remove from the heat and keep warm.

6 Transfer the chicken legs to a bowl and let cool slightly. Once they are cool enough to handle, use two forks to shred the meat and discard the skin and bones. Stir the shredded chicken, dill, and lemon zest into the soup, then taste and adjust the seasoning with salt and pepper.

7 Using a slotted spoon, transfer the cooked matzo balls to serving bowls, then ladle the soup over and serve.

Persian Beef, Herb, and Kidney Bean Stew (Khoresh-e Ghormeh Sabzi)

YIELD: SERVES 8 TO 10

PREP TIME: 30 MINUTES, PLUS OVERNIGHT SOAKING AND CHILLING TIME

COOK TIME: 2 HOURS 30 MINUTES

Early into my relationship with Alex, this classic Persian stew was one of my first ventures into the world of the Iranian dishes he grew up eating. Packed with whole bunches of chopped parsley, cilantro, and scallions, *ghormeh sabzi* simmers red kidney beans and meat in a flavorful broth of dried Persian limes for the perfect combination of richness and brightness. It's perfect for a cold winter night, for making use of a fresh spring herb haul, or for any occasion where a bit of comfort food is required. Just make sure to have plenty of Shirazi salad (page 88), *mast-o-khiar* (page 55), and *tahdig* (page 132) on hand, and you're ready to party.

This recipe will require shopping for two potentially foreign ingredients at a specialty spice store or online: dried fenugreek leaves and dried black Persian limes (*limu omani*). Fenugreek leaves (separate from fenugreek seeds) are vibrantly floral with hints of anise and celery flavor and an aroma of maple syrup. You're not adding enough to give it dominance in flavor, but a tablespoon rounds out the stew to offer balance to the tang introduced by our second provision. Much like their name hints, dried Persian limes are made by, well, drying whole limes in the sun until black. Instead of just adding acidity, dried limes add a complex lip-smacking sourness that absolutely cannot be replicated by anything else, so don't even try asking me for a substitution!

As when preparing any braise, it's very important to chill out. For best result, the stew should be cooked completely and chilled overnight, then reheated and served. That way, you not only give the flavors time to meld and the dried lime the opportunity to infuse the dish, but also activate the gelatin from the beef and the starch from the kidney beans to give the stew the body you want. If I'm cooking this dish for a party, I make it anywhere from one to three nights in advance. Then all I have to do is throw it on the stove to reheat before serving.

RECIPE CONTINUES

3 tablespoons vegetable oil

3 pounds beef chuck, cut into 1½-inch pieces

Kosher salt and freshly ground black pepper

1 medium yellow onion, chopped

1 tablespoon dried fenugreek leaves

1 tablespoon ground turmeric

12 scallions, minced

4 cups packed fresh parsley leaves and tender stems, minced

4 cups packed fresh cilantro leaves and tender stems, minced

4 cups chicken stock

2 cups dried red kidney beans, soaked overnight and drained (see tip)

6 dried black Persian limes

Rice, preferably tahdig (page 132), for serving

1 In a large Dutch oven or pot, heat the oil over medium-high heat. Season the beef with a heavy pinch each of salt and pepper. Working in two batches, sear the beef, turning it as needed, until golden brown, 8 to 10 minutes per batch. Transfer the seared beef to a bowl.

2 Add the onion to the pot and cook, stirring often, until softened and lightly caramelized, 3 to 4 minutes. Stir in the fenugreek and turmeric and cook until fragrant, about 1 minute. Add the scallions, parsley, and cilantro to the pot and cook, stirring continuously with a wooden spoon and scraping up any browned bits on the bottom of the pot, until the herbs are dark green in color, 4 to 5 minutes.

3 Add the seared beef, stock, beans, dried limes, and 2 cups water, then bring to a light simmer, reducing the heat as needed. Cover and cook until both the beef and the beans are very tender, about 2 hours. Halfway through cooking, use a paring knife to carefully pierce a hole in each dried lime to release their flavor into the stew. Taste and adjust the seasoning with salt and pepper. For the best consistency and flavor, let the stew cool completely and refrigerate overnight.

4 The next day, reheat the stew over medium heat until warm. Taste and adjust the seasoning again with salt and pepper, then serve with rice.

Soaking Beans! Whenever a recipe calls for beans to be soaked overnight, it means that the night before (or at least 8 hours before) you'd like to cook the recipe, you need to put the beans in a large bowl and add cool water to cover by 3 inches. Cover the bowl and set aside to soak at room temperature. The next day, you'll find that the beans have soaked up some of the water and plumped up dramatically, which will help them cook faster and evenly.

Forgot to soak your beans? Or just don't want to? Quick soak your beans! Put the beans in a medium saucepan and add cool water to cover by at least 2 inches. Bring to a boil over high heat, then cook for 5 minutes. Remove from the heat and let sit for 1 hour, then drain and proceed with the recipe!

Persian Chicken and Celery Stew (Khoresh-e Karafs)

YIELD: SERVES 8 TO 10

PREP TIME: 20 MINUTES

COOK TIME: 1 HOUR 20 MINUTES

3 tablespoons vegetable oil

3 pounds boneless, skinless chicken thighs, cut into 1½-inch pieces and patted dry

Kosher salt and freshly ground black pepper

2 medium yellow onions, chopped

2 teaspoons ground cumin

½ teaspoon ground cinnamon

¼ teaspoon ground cardamom

4 cups chicken stock

2 pounds celery (1 bunch), leaves removed and reserved

2 tablespoons freshly squeezed lime juice

1 tablespoon packed light brown sugar

Rice, preferably tahdig (page 132), for serving

Celery is the Cinderella of vegetables, hidden as tiny pieces or in purees, spending its days living in the shadow of trendier produce. But dressed up in a fragrant Persian stew with warm spices and chicken, celery becomes the belle of the ball. My mother-in-law makes a big pot of *khoresh-e karafs* whenever we come to visit, and I have been known to eat it for breakfast, lunch, and dinner during our stays. A simple base of onions, cumin, and cinnamon is transformed at the very end when sliced celery is added, imparting a delicate, verdant flavor and a toothsome bite to the dish. The celery adds levity to an otherwise heavy stew, making it very easy to eat with abandon.

While Robina makes hers with beef, I already used that for the *ghormeh sabzi* on page 149, so I tried a version with chicken thighs to see how they would hold up. Needless to say, not only did it pack the same power, but the stew cooked in less time for a taste of Persian comfort food without hours chained to the stove. And given the fibrous nature of celery, it's a recipe that even freezes beautifully, losing no integrity when defrosted.

The moral of the story is: Don't sleep on celery. I'm no fairy godmother—well, I'm no godmother—but you'll just have to take my word that this creation is nothing short of magic.

1 In a large Dutch oven, heat the oil over medium-high heat. Season the chicken with a heavy pinch each of salt and pepper. Working in two batches, sear the chicken, turning it as needed, until golden brown, 8 to 10 minutes per batch. Transfer the seared chicken to a bowl.

2 Add the onions to the pot and cook, stirring continuously with a wooden spoon and scraping up any browned bits on the bottom of the pot, until softened and lightly caramelized, 3 to 4 minutes. Stir in the cumin, cin-namon, and cardamom and cook until fragrant, about 1 minute.

3 Add the seared chicken, stock, and a heavy pinch each of salt and pep-per, then bring to a simmer. Cover the pot with the lid ajar and cook until the chicken is very tender, 40 to 45 minutes.

4 Meanwhile, slice the celery stalks ¼ inch thick on an angle.

5 Once the chicken is tender, stir in the sliced celery, lime juice, and brown sugar. Return the mixture to a simmer and cook until the celery is tender but not mushy, 15 to 20 minutes more. Remove from the heat. Taste and adjust the seasoning with salt and pepper. Garnish with the reserved celery leaves, then serve with rice. (Alternatively, let cool completely and refrigerate overnight, since this stew tastes even better reheated the next day.)

a tale of two briskets

Brisket is political. You may think of it as a cozy braise, but it's so much more. It's a vessel of family pride and tradition. A consistent comfort food made for any celebratory occasion. Gentiles may have family crests, but Jews have family brisket recipes. Everything I know about brisket I learned from my aunt Susi. Growing up, she would host the High Holidays in her apartment, where an extremely worn Le Creuset Dutch oven filled with brisket bubbling in tomato sauce sat on her crowded stovetop. Silver platters were passed around, perfuming the room with the aromas of bay leaves and garlic, as everyone showered Susi with compliments.

After a lifetime of this dish, the intricacies of braised diplomacy became clear the first time I helped my sister-in-law Leigh cook her Passover seder, a few months into dating Alex. I took on cooking 18 pounds of brisket for the thirty people coming to celebrate. I seared each giant slab before caramelizing onions and mushrooms to become the base of the red wine–spiked tomato sauce. Fresh bay leaves were nestled into the pan, along with a garden of sage, rosemary, and thyme. This was my first holiday with Alex's family, and everything had to be perfect. And it was. It was perfectly tender, with the perfect balance of umami from the mushrooms, sweetness from the carrots, and acidity from the tomatoes and wine. Alex still talks about it. I still dream about it.

However, it was not the *Fisher family* brisket, and I was stripped of brisket duty the following year so their version could return. Their brisket is braised with peppers, mirepoix, and red wine, then covered in a sauce made by pureeing all the vegetables with the braising liquid. It was delicious, but nothing like what I knew of brisket. I had never had brisket without tomatoes. But this was only the beginning of my brisket renaissance, as I continued in my career,

testing and adapting recipes from chefs and food writers far and near. I've seen the full spectrum of briskets, from those laced with dried porcinis for an ultra-savory punch to three-ingredient versions that only use onions and a giant bottle of ketchup (both are equally lovely).

Instead of shaming other families for their brisket choices, you have to step back to see how it's simply a beautiful representation of the evolution of Diaspora cuisine. Ashkenazi families, with their love of brisket, scattered across the world when they left Europe. For those who landed in the States, their recipes continued to be transformed as they used ingredients available here, catapulting brisket into the canon of American Jewish culinary traditions.

It's with this in mind that I offer you the two recipes for brisket that I live by. The first is a zhuzhed-up version of Susi's brisket. Instead of tomato sauce, I roast canned whole peeled tomatoes until caramelized, then mash them up to join caramelized onions and mushrooms, a healthy glug of red wine, and plenty of aromatics. It's the recipe I serve at so many of my Shabbats because it's a comforting crowd-pleaser, but also because, for me, nothing represents hospitality like serving a dish that literally took days to make. The second recipe is my way of taking poetic license with brisket, drawing inspiration from French onion soup for a braising liquid of caramelized onions and garlic, deglazed with apple brandy. Funny enough, my sister has betrayed the family and currently pledges her allegiance to my French onion brisket.

I've now taken over for Susi in preparing the brisket for the holidays, which has come with its own set of expectations. Well, actually, there's only one responsibility no matter which recipe you follow: make enough for leftovers.

Roasted Tomato Brisket

YIELD: SERVES 10 TO 12

PREP TIME: 20 MINUTES, PLUS COOLING TIME AND OVERNIGHT CHILLING

COOK TIME: 4 HOURS

2 (28-ounce) cans whole peeled tomatoes

4 tablespoons extra-virgin olive oil

1 (5- to 6-pound) beef brisket, fat cap intact (see tip, page 159)

Kosher salt and freshly ground black pepper

12 ounces cremini mushrooms, thinly sliced (2 cups)

2 large yellow onions, diced

6 garlic cloves, smashed and peeled

1 cup red wine

2 large carrots, scrubbed and cut into 1-inch pieces

12 sprigs thyme

4 fresh bay leaves

1 Preheat the oven to 450°F.

2 Pour the canned tomatoes and all their liquid into a 9 by 13-inch baking dish and spread them into an even layer. Drizzle 1 tablespoon of the olive oil on top. Roast for 30 minutes. Move the dish to the top rack of the oven, then turn on the broiler and broil for 3 to 4 minutes, until tops of the tomatoes begin to lightly char. Remove from the oven and let cool slightly, then carefully mash the tomatoes with the back of a fork or a potato masher. Reduce the oven temperature to 325°F.

3 Season each side of the brisket with 2 heavy pinches each of salt and pepper. In a large Dutch oven, heat the remaining 3 tablespoons olive oil over medium-high heat. Sear the brisket, turning it as needed, until golden brown, 15 to 20 minutes (see tip, page 159). Transfer the brisket to a platter.

4 Reduce the heat to medium, then add the mushrooms, onions, and garlic to the pot. Cook, stirring often, until softened and lightly caramelized, 10 to 15 minutes. Add the wine, then stir continuously with a wooden spoon for 1 minute to scrape up any browned bits on the bottom of the pot.

5 Stir in the roasted tomatoes, carrots, and 2 heavy pinches each of salt and pepper, then return the brisket to the pot. Tie together the thyme sprigs and bay leaves with a small piece of butcher's twine (tying is optional, but makes it much easier to remove the herbs after cooking) and nestle the herb bundle in the pot. Bring to a simmer, then cover the pot and transfer to the oven. Cook for 3 hours to 3 hours 30 minutes, until very tender when pierced with a fork. Remove from the oven and let cool completely, then refrigerate overnight.

6 The next day, skim off and discard any fat, if desired, and discard the herbs. Transfer the brisket to a cutting board and cut it across the grain (perpendicular to the fibers you'll see running through the brisket) into ¼-inch-thick slices. Return the meat to the sauce and heat over medium heat until warmed through. Taste and adjust the seasoning with salt and pepper, then serve.

! **Brisket Pasta** These recipes are delicious, but while everyone is fighting over the meat, I'm just thinking about the sauce. I save all the braising liquid, packed with lil' bits of fallen-apart meat, and use it as the king of pasta sauces. It's truly better than any ragù or Sunday gravy you could dream of. Simply cook pasta (rotini is my go-to!) until it's *just* al dente, then drain and drop into a simmering pot of a few cups of the leftover braising liquid to finish cooking and let the liquid reduce down to coat the noodles. If you're feeling wild, finish it off by making it rain Parmesan!!

French Onion Brisket

YIELD: SERVES 10 TO 12

PREP TIME: 20 MINUTES, PLUS COOLING TIME AND OVERNIGHT CHILLING

COOK TIME: 3 HOURS 40 MINUTES

1 (5- to 6-pound) beef brisket, fat cap intact (see tip)

Kosher salt and freshly ground black pepper

3 tablespoons vegetable oil

5 large sweet onions, thinly sliced

12 garlic cloves, smashed and peeled

1 cup Calvados or sherry

3 cups chicken stock

6 sprigs thyme

4 sprigs sage

1 Preheat the oven to 325°F.

2 Season each side of the brisket with 2 heavy pinches each of salt and pepper. In a large Dutch oven, heat the oil over medium-high heat. Sear the brisket, turning it as needed, until golden brown, 15 to 20 minutes (see tip). Transfer the brisket to a platter.

3 Reduce the heat to medium, then add the onions and garlic to the pot. Cook, stirring often, until softened and caramelized, 20 to 25 minutes. Add the Calvados, then stir continuously with a wooden spoon for 1 minute to scrape up any browned bits on the bottom of the pot.

4 Stir in the stock and 2 heavy pinches each of salt and pepper, then return the brisket to pot. Tie together the thyme and sage sprigs with a small piece of butcher's twine (tying is optional, but makes it much easier to remove the herbs after cooking) and nestle the herb bundle in the pot. Bring to a simmer, then cover the pot and transfer it to the oven. Cook for 3 hours to 3 hours 30 minutes, until very tender when pierced with a fork. Remove from the oven and let cool completely, then refrigerate overnight.

5 The next day, skim off and discard any fat, if desired, and discard the herbs. Transfer the brisket to a cutting board and cut it across the grain (perpendicular to the fibers you'll see running through the brisket) into ¼-inch-thick slices. Return the meat to the sauce and heat over medium heat until warmed through. Taste and adjust the seasoning with salt and pepper, then serve.

Buying Brisket 101 Beef briskets come in many shapes and sizes (just like us!), but it all comes down to choosing between the first (or flat) cut and the second (or point) cut. The flat is much leaner, and often smaller, made up of one muscle cleaned of most fat. The point, my preferred cut, contains the deckle, a gorgeous layer of the fat and muscle attached the rib cage. More fat equals more flavor, so don't deprive yourself of the deckle! As for the size, I find 5 to 6 pounds is the sweet spot for yielding a ton of brisket while still being manageable for even my tiny NYC kitchen.

Make It Fit! Now, let's just say you're really struggling to make a whole brisket fit in your Dutch oven and a new one just isn't in your budget. You can 100 percent halve the brisket crosswise to make it more manageable. Just sear it off in batches before braising, and it will still be delicious (and even cook slightly faster). But if you can keep it whole, that's still the best-case scenario for a low-and-slow buildup of flavor!

hanukkah

Crack out the gelt, because this is the only way I eat on Hanukkah. Grease lightning!

———

mains

Herb-Roasted Spatchcocked Chicken

YIELD: SERVES 4

PREP TIME: 20 MINUTES, PLUS
RESTING TIME

COOK TIME: 1 HOUR

1 pound Yukon Gold potatoes, scrubbed
and sliced ¼ inch thick

1 medium yellow onion, thinly sliced

⅓ cup Compound Schmaltz (page 6), at
room temperature

Kosher salt

1 (4½-pound) whole chicken, spatchcocked (see tip)

¾ cup chicken stock

WWIGD? What would Ina Garten do? Nine times out of ten, no matter what the question, the answer is "roast a chicken." As I structure my life around becoming the gay Ina (with Alex as my Jeffrey), naturally there is a lot of poultry involved. We love a good pan-seared thigh, but there's nothing quite like roasting the entire bird. There's no need to truss it, as I've become a serial spatchcocker, since it speeds up the roasting time for more last-minute chicken dinners.

I'll gladly pass along my trick for achieving that heavenly crispy skin that you'll want to pick off and eat before any of your guests arrive. It's schmaltz. If you've never worked with rendered chicken fat before, it's about time you did. I rub a compound schmaltz laced with herbs and garlic under the skin and all over the chicken so it practically confits itself in the oven. And if that isn't reason enough to make this recipe, all that schmaltzy goodness (a technical term) then drips over sliced potatoes and onions. *Oomph* You too can achieve Ina-level poultry perfection—I believe in you!

! **How to Spatchcock** Use strong kitchen shears to cut along both sides of the backbone to remove it completely. Set the chicken skin-side down, open the cavity, and make a small cut in the breastbone (you're not looking to cut through all the way). Flip the chicken over (skin-side up) and use the palm of your hand to press on the breastbone and flatten the chicken. Tuck the wing tips under so they don't burn.

1 Preheat the oven to 450°F.

2 In a large cast-iron skillet, toss the potatoes and onion with 2 tablespoons of the schmaltz and a heavy pinch of salt. Spread in an even layer and top with the spatchcocked chicken, skin-side up. Rub the chicken with the remaining schmaltz, both under the skin and over it, then season with a heavy pinch of salt.

3 Roast the chicken for 30 minutes, then pour the stock into the pan,

making sure not to pour it directly onto the chicken. Roast for 15 to 20 minutes more, until the chicken is golden brown and a thermometer reads 165°F when inserted into the center of the breast and thigh.

4 Remove from the oven. Let the chicken rest for 10 minutes, then carve and serve over the potatoes and onion.

Iraqi Roasted Salmon with Tomato and Lemon

YIELD: SERVES 8 TO 10
PREP TIME: 20 MINUTES
COOK TIME: 30 MINUTES

3 tablespoons extra-virgin olive oil

2 medium yellow onions, minced

2 scallions, white and green parts separated and thinly sliced

2 teaspoons ground coriander

1 teaspoon ground cumin

1 teaspoon ground turmeric

½ teaspoon cayenne pepper

1 (6-ounce) can tomato paste

2 teaspoons finely grated lemon zest

Kosher salt

1 (3-pound) whole side of salmon, skin-on

Lemon wedges, for serving

This dish is truly an awakening of flavor. As soon as you make it, it's damn near impossible to go back to preparing salmon any other way. I learned the recipe via detailed phone calls with Alex's mother Robina, who inherited it from her mother Evelyn, or Mama Eva as she was called. Smothered in onions and caramelized tomato paste, the salmon sings with bright acidity from lemon and heat from Iraqi curry powder (which I've simplified here with coriander, cumin, turmeric, and cayenne). When it's done, I throw some sliced scallions on top and put it straight on the table. It's just as easy as it is popular, so get ready to join the fan club!

As this has become a true Shabbat staple in my house, here's how to make your life even easier. Go ahead and make the tomato-onion mixture up to a few days in advance. It also freezes beautifully, so typically, if I'm taking the time to caramelize onions and tomato paste, I'll double the quantities and freeze half so I'm stocked up for the next time I make this salmon. The recipe originally called for an entire fish, but I adapted it to use a whole side of salmon to make it a little more accessible. Now, if you're looking to make less than an entire side of salmon, just use individual fillets and spoon a few tablespoons of the mixture over the top before popping it into the oven. Just be sure to line your pan with foil for easy cleanup.

1 Preheat the oven to 475°F. Line a half sheet pan with aluminum foil.

2 In a medium skillet, heat the olive oil over medium-high heat. Add the onions and scallion whites and cook, stirring often, until softened and lightly caramelized, 10 to 12 minutes. Stir in the coriander, cumin, turmeric, and cayenne and cook, stirring continuously, until fragrant, about 1 minute.

3 Stir in the tomato paste and cook, stirring often, until well incorporated and caramelized to the color of rust, 3 to 4 minutes. Remove from the heat and stir in the lemon zest. Season with salt and let cool slightly.

4 Place the side of salmon on the prepared sheet pan, skin-side down (and arranged diagonally to fit, if necessary), and season with a heavy pinch of salt. Spread the tomato mixture over the top of the salmon in an even layer. Roast for 15 to 20 minutes, until the salmon is golden and reaches an internal temperature of 145°F. (If desired, broil the salmon for 2 to 3 minutes to get more color.)

5 Garnish the salmon with the scallion greens, then serve with lemon wedges.

Lemony Sheet Pan Chicken
with Crispy Chickpeas and Kale

YIELD: SERVES 4 TO 6

PREP TIME: 15 MINUTES, PLUS 4 HOURS MARINATING TIME

COOK TIME: 35 MINUTES

2 pounds whole bone-in, skin-on chicken legs (4 medium)

1 (15-ounce) can chickpeas, drained

4 tablespoons extra-virgin olive oil

¼ cup finely chopped preserved lemons

1½ teaspoons kosher salt, plus more as needed

½ teaspoon dried oregano

½ teaspoon Aleppo pepper or crushed red pepper

12 ounces lacinato kale, leaves stemmed and roughly torn

So much of what I cook at home is made up of comforting dishes focused on simple ingredients with one curveball snuck in. For this chicken dinner winner, it's all about the preserved lemons. If you've never tried this magical North African ingredient, it's the ray of sunshine your kitchen pantry is missing. Lemons are packed with salt, then left to pickle as the salt slowly pulls the juice from the lemons to make their own brine. The skins soften and take on a level of floral citrusy flavor that's unlike the flavor of the fresh stuff. In this recipe, preserved lemons add some tang and vibrance to chicken legs and chickpeas, which get roasted until golden and crisp. Throw on some kale for the last few minutes, and you've got yourself a healthy supper in no time.

Okay, I lied. There's another curveball: Aleppo pepper. This Syrian crushed chile beautifully adds color and heat to any dish, though crushed red pepper will do the trick instead. The preserved lemons, however, are nonnegotiable. Let's say you really can't find any after scouring specialty stores and the internet (I don't believe you) and don't have time to make them yourself (it only takes about a month to DIY)—well, then I guess you can substitute the finely grated zest and juice of 1 lemon, but it won't be the same!

1 In a resealable bag or large bowl, toss the chicken, chickpeas, 3 tablespoons of the olive oil, the preserved lemons, salt, oregano, and Aleppo pepper to coat. Refrigerate for at least 4 hours or preferably overnight to marinate.

2 Once the chicken is marinated, preheat the oven to 450°F.

3 Transfer the chicken mixture to a half sheet pan, spreading it into an even layer and placing the legs skin-side up. Season the legs with a pinch more salt. Roast for about 30 minutes, until the chicken is golden and the chickpeas are crisp.

4 Meanwhile, in a medium bowl, massage the kale with the remaining

1 tablespoon olive oil and a heavy pinch of salt.

5 After the chicken has roasted for 30 minutes, add the kale to the pan, spreading it evenly around the chicken legs. Roast for about 5 minutes, until the kale has wilted and the thighs have reached an internal temperature of 165°F.

6 Remove from the oven and let the chicken rest on the pan for 5 minutes. Transfer the chicken legs to a cutting board and carve, separating the thighs from the drumsticks. Transfer the kale and chickpea mixture to a platter, top with the chicken pieces, and serve.

Crispy Chicken Thighs with Tzimmes

YIELD: SERVES 4

PREP TIME: 20 MINUTES

COOK TIME: 40 MINUTES

2 pounds bone-in, skin-on chicken thighs (4 medium), patted dry

2 teaspoons finely grated orange zest

1 teaspoon ground cinnamon

Kosher salt and freshly ground black pepper

5 tablespoons extra-virgin olive oil

1 medium yellow onion, thinly sliced

1½ pounds rainbow carrots with green tops, cut into 2-inch pieces, tops reserved

1 cup dried prunes, coarsely chopped

½ cup freshly squeezed orange juice

¾ cup chicken stock

1 garlic clove, finely grated

We weren't allowed dark meat in my household growing up. My mother was scarred from her own childhood, where white meat was reserved for the men, and made a promise to herself that her children would only have chicken breasts in an attempt to overthrow the patriarchy! The twist? My sister and I both prefer dark meat, of course. Crispy chicken thighs have become a weeknight staple in my kitchen, where I render every ounce of chicken fat from the skin and use it to cook a seasonal mix of veggies.

This fall version adds on another classic Jewish dish, tzimmes, a sweet-and-sour side dish of carrots and sometimes other root veggies cooked with dried fruit. Perfumed with orange zest and cinnamon, the chicken thighs roast over a bed of carrots and prunes (shout-out to the Jewish people's favorite and necessary snack!), allowing all the juices to collect in the pan and steam the vegetables in the oven. To add a little zing, the carrot tops are saved and chopped up with garlic and olive oil for a relish that helps liven the whole thing up.

1 Preheat the oven to 400°F.

2 In a large bowl, toss the chicken thighs with 1 teaspoon of the orange zest, ½ teaspoon of the cinnamon, and a heavy pinch each of salt and pepper to coat.

3 In a large ovenproof skillet, heat 3 tablespoons of the olive oil over medium heat. Place the thighs in the pan, skin-side down, and cook until the skin is golden and the fat has rendered, 8 to 10 minutes. Flip the thighs and cook to sear the other side, 3 to 4 minutes. Transfer to a plate.

4 Raise the heat to medium-high, then add the onion to the skillet. Cook, stirring often, until softened and lightly caramelized, 3 to 4 minutes. Stir in the remaining 1 teaspoon orange zest and ½ teaspoon cinnamon to incorporate.

Add the carrots, followed by the prunes and orange juice, and cook, stirring often, until the carrots begin to soften and the orange juice glazes them, 10 to 12 minutes.

5 Stir in the stock and season with a heavy pinch each of salt and pepper. Place the thighs on top, skin-side up, and transfer the skillet to the oven. Roast for 15 minutes, until the thighs have reached an internal temperature of 165°F and the carrots are tender.

6 Meanwhile, coarsely chop 2 cups of the reserved carrot greens and put them in a small bowl. Add the garlic and remaining 2 tablespoons olive oil and stir to combine. Season with salt and pepper.

7 Spoon the carrot-top relish over the chicken and carrots, then serve.

Harissa-Marinated Grilled Flank Steak and Summer Vegetables

YIELD: SERVES 4 TO 6

PREP TIME: 20 MINUTES, PLUS 4 HOURS MARINATING TIME

COOK TIME: 25 MINUTES

¼ cup harissa

¼ cup extra-virgin olive oil

¼ cup packed light brown sugar

Grated zest and juice of 1 orange

1 tablespoon kosher salt

1 (2-pound) flank steak

3 small zucchini, halved lengthwise

2 red bell peppers, quartered

1 medium eggplant, cut into 1-inch-thick slices

1 medium red onion, cut into wedges

Flaky sea salt, for garnish

I love working on vacation. Well, not working, per se, but still chained to the kitchen. Every year in August, we try to get away from the disgustingly sweaty city as often as we can, and spend as much time as possible with Alex's family in northern Connecticut, where his brother and sister-in-law rent a house. And while you'd think I'd want to just relax by the pool and eat hot dogs with abandon (don't worry, plenty of that is done), I find myself spending most of my days cooking and baking. I kid you not, I even pack up half my pantry to bring with me to ensure I have all my favorite essentials in this foreign kitchen.

One fateful summer Friday, my heart was set on a grill-out Shabbat. The challah dough was proofing poolside while I ventured to the local farm stand for a bounty of flowering squash, plump eggplant, almost-fluorescent-y-vibrant peppers, and a giant flank steak. Naturally, I raided my traveling pantry to get these beauties all dressed for the Sabbath grill. Equal parts smoky North African harissa, olive oil, and brown sugar are met with a heavy dash of salt and the zest and juice of an orange for a simple marinade that gives a little sugar-and-spice to anything it touches.

Think of this recipe as a blueprint for the marinade, so let me answer some hypothetical FAQs. Yes, you can swap in your favorite cut of steak, and mix and match the vegetables! Yes, it will work with chicken! No, you should not use less than 1 tablespoon salt! Yes, you should double the marinade if you're cooking 4 pounds of steak! Yes, you can even use this marinade if you're skipping the grill entirely to roast the veg in the oven and cook the steak on the stove instead!

1 In a large bowl, whisk together the harissa, olive oil, brown sugar, orange zest, orange juice, and kosher salt until smooth.

2 Add the steak, zucchini, bell peppers, eggplant, and onion and toss to coat. Cover and refrigerate for at least 4 hours or preferably overnight to marinate.

3 When the steak and vegetables have marinated, heat a grill to medium-high.

4 Remove the steak and vegetables from the marinade and pat dry with paper towels. Grill the vegetables, concentrating them to two-thirds of the grill's surface and turning them as needed, until lightly charred and tender, 8 to 10 minutes. As the vegetables are finished, transfer them to a platter and tent with aluminum foil to keep warm.

5 Meanwhile, grill the steak on the empty portion of the grill, flipping it once, until golden brown and a thermometer inserted into the center reads 125°F (for medium-rare), 5 to 6 minutes per side. Transfer the steak to a cutting board and let rest for 10 minutes, then slice it across the grain (perpendicular to the fibers you'll see running through the steak) and place it over the grilled vegetables. Garnish with flaky sea salt, then serve.

Lamb Chops with Crushed Grapes and Sage

YIELD: SERVES 4

PREP TIME: 20 MINUTES, PLUS OVERNIGHT MARINATING TIME

COOK TIME: 20 MINUTES

4 cups stemmed seedless green grapes

4 garlic cloves, smashed and peeled

5 sprigs sage

2 pounds boneless lamb shoulder chops (6 medium)

4 tablespoons extra-virgin olive oil

2 teaspoons kosher salt, plus more as needed

1 teaspoon freshly ground black pepper, plus more as needed

When it came to our wedding, nothing said "love wins" like ignoring all family input and getting our own way. Alex and I wanted an intimate celebration that focused on the two things we prioritize most: food and family. That meant keeping it small and inviting only our closest loved ones. That meant no choosing between mediocre chicken and mediocre salmon. That meant no dry-ass wedding cake. We ended up with the most sensational reception with seventy people at Sunday in Brooklyn, our favorite restaurant in NYC, where we served fried chicken, pastrami cod, perfectly medium-rare steak, and the most gorgeous wedding cake from Dominique Ansel.

Even with such a magical wedding, I still consider our anniversary to be the day before. In lieu of a rehearsal dinner, we gathered our immediate families at Alex's brother's apartment to join us as we signed our ketubah, the Jewish marriage license, with our rabbi. With our mothers as our witnesses and our fathers holding a tallit overhead for a makeshift chuppah, it couldn't have been a more meaningful celebration of our love. The evening concluded with an Israeli feast at Miznon in Chelsea Market. As waiters passed around shots of arak, we sanctified our marriage with never-ending platters of pita, whole roasted cauliflower, and the most incredible roasted leg of lamb, which inspired this recipe.

Simply marinated in crushed green grapes and sage and sporting the perfect balance of caramelized sweetness and earthy funk, the lamb was unlike anything I'd ever had. I've adapted this concept for lamb chops, which are a bit more approachable for casual entertaining and customizing to your number of guests. If you want to ball out on frenched rib chops, by all means, treat yourself! However, I've fallen in love with lamb shoulder chops, which are more affordable and just as tender when left bathing in this flavorful marinade. Served with roasted grapes, this recipe is not only delicious, it's gay rights!

1 In a large bowl, combine 2 cups of the grapes, the garlic, and the sage. Using a potato masher or the back of a fork, mash until the grapes have broken down to a pulp and the sage is bruised. Add the lamb chops, 2 tablespoons of the olive oil, the salt, and the pepper, then toss to coat. Cover and refrigerate overnight.

2 The next day, preheat the oven to 425°F.

RECIPE CONTINUES

3 Remove the lamb chops from the marinade and pat dry with paper towels. Pour the marinade into a heatproof casserole dish, add the remaining 2 cups whole grapes, and toss to coat. Roast the grapes for 15 to 20 minutes, until tender and golden.

4 Meanwhile, in a large cast-iron skillet, heat the remaining 2 tablespoons olive oil over medium-high heat. Season the lamb chops with a heavy pinch each of salt and pepper. Working with half the chops, cook, flipping them once, until golden and medium-rare, 3 to 4 minutes per side. Transfer to a platter, tent with aluminum foil, and let rest as you cook the second batch.

5 Once all the lamb chops are cooked, spoon the roasted grape mixture over them, then serve.

Eggplant Dolmeh
(Beef-Stuffed Eggplant)

YIELD: SERVES 8 TO 10

PREP TIME: 35 MINUTES

COOK TIME: 55 MINUTES

¾ cup panko bread crumbs

1 medium yellow onion, coarsely grated

2 pounds ground beef

2 teaspoons kosher salt, plus more as needed

2 teaspoons ground cumin

1 teaspoon freshly ground black pepper, plus more as needed

¼ teaspoon cayenne pepper

2 medium eggplants, preferably with an elongated shape

4 large eggs

Vegetable oil, for frying

2 cups tomato puree

¼ cup tamarind concentrate, or 2 tablespoons freshly squeezed lemon juice

1 tablespoon sugar

2 ounces feta cheese, crumbled, for garnish

2 tablespoons chopped fresh parsley, for garnish

There are two types of people in this world: those who can eat the same thing every day for a week, and those who need constant variety. While I'm typically one to switch up what's on the menu daily, I make an annual concession when we visit Alex's parents in Florida. My mother-in-law, Robina, starts cooking weeks in advance, preparing at least 10 pounds of beef divided between a batch of *ghormeh sabzi* (page 149), *khoresh-e karafs* (see page 152 for my version with chicken), and a couple of trays of these life-changing *dolmeh*. I swear there have been four-day spans in which I ate these *dolmeh* for breakfast, lunch, and dinner.

While most Middle Eastern cultures have some form of *dolmeh,* or stuffed vegetables, this variation is a mash-up of the recipe Robina learned from her ex-mother-in-law in Turkey, with ingredients like tamarind, which is popular with the Iraqi Jewish community from their involvement in the spice trade with India. Slices of fried eggplant are rolled up around a mixture of ground beef seasoned with cumin and grated onion, then baked in a tamarind-tinted tomato sauce. In the oven, the juices of the *dolmeh* melt into the sauce, which then gets sucked back into each rollup like a sponge. It's sweet, tangy, and, according to me, great at any time of day.

1 Preheat the oven to 425°F. Line a half sheet pan with paper towels.

2 In a large bowl, stir together the panko and grated onion to make a paste. Add the beef, salt, cumin, black pepper, and cayenne. Using your hands, mix until well incorporated.

3 Trim the tops and bottoms of each eggplant, then cut them lengthwise into ¼-inch-thick slices.

4 In a large bowl, whisk the eggs with a heavy pinch each of salt and pepper until smooth. Add the eggplant slices and toss to coat completely. Transfer the slices to a colander set over a bowl and let drain for 5 minutes.

5 In a large cast-iron or nonstick skillet, heat a thin layer of oil over medium-high heat until shimmering. Working in batches, fry a few slices of the eggplant at a time, flipping them

once, until golden and softened, about 2 minutes per side. Transfer to the paper towel–lined pan to drain. Repeat with the remaining eggplant slices, adding more oil to the pan as needed between batches, until all the eggplant has been fried. Let cool slightly.

6 Place 2 tablespoons of the beef mixture at the base of each eggplant slice and roll up the eggplant length-wise to enclose the filling. Place the rolls seam-side down in a 9 by 13-inch baking dish.

7 In a medium bowl, stir together the tomato puree, tamarind concentrate, sugar, and ½ cup water. Season with salt and pepper, then pour the mixture over the eggplant rolls to coat. Bake for 35 to 40 minutes, until the edges of the eggplant rolls are golden.

8 Remove from the oven. Garnish with the feta and parsley, then serve.

you
can't
beat

a babka!

My obsession with babka began when I met Alex, for the simple reason that he didn't know what babka was. As an Iraqi Jew, Alex moved to New York with zero knowledge of Ashkenazi foods, sparking my need to educate him in everything from babka and bialys to matzo balls and Manischewitz. I got to watch with glee as he gummed his first piece of gefilte fish at a seder, dumbfounded over our menu, which didn't include any of the fragrant rices or stews of his childhood. Did he like it? Not really. But that wasn't the point! In the same way that I've completely immersed myself in Iraqi and Persian Jewish food culture, I wanted to expose him to the Eastern-European-New-York-Jewish staples I grew up on. We were beginning to forge our relationship and combine not only families but family traditions, so these exchanges were part of our unique narrative as a modern Jewish couple. There have been hits and misses when it comes to our adventures introducing Alex to Ashkenazi food, but nothing slaps quite like babka.

The first time I made it for him was while I was working in the test kitchen at *Saveur* magazine. I was testing Leah Koenig's raspberry-glazed chocolate babka from *Modern Jewish Cooking* the same day we were leaving for Puerto Rico, our first vacation together, so I wrapped a loaf in plastic and shoved it in my backpack. That evening, when we arrived at the hotel room we were sharing with two of Alex's friends (budget travel!!) in San Juan, we woke them up to join us in a late-night dinner of babka. As crumbs spilled all over the bed, we crushed the entire thing, and Alex and his friends were mesmerized by this foreign creation. Long story short, the flight back to New York was when we first told each other "I love you." I'm not saying it was because of babka, but it definitely sanctified the dish in our relationship in the sweetest way possible.

Past the gushy romantic stuff, what makes babka so beautiful is how customizable it is. Long gone are the days of *Seinfeld*, when your only choices were chocolate or cinnamon! After tweaking and perfecting my base dough, I began pushing the boundaries of what I could twist between these fluffy layers: Silky tahini was swirled into chocolate ganache, cinnamon was used to spice a pumpkin filling for a fall-baking vibe, and I entered the magical world of savory babkas, spreading pistachio pesto studded with sun-dried tomatoes on the dough and even baking a loaf packed with all the flavors of the classic reuben.

If it's your first time making babka, I pass on to you my pearls of wisdom as someone who has persevered after slicing into dry loaves many times, as well as loaves that were still raw in the middle! You need to respect the dough. This ain't a no-knead baking project. Since you're going to have a softer dough than you might be used to, you want to make sure you mix it enough to build up a proper gluten structure. Then, don't skimp on the proof. If you want a fluffy babka, make sure you give it the time to rise; how long it needs will fluctuate depending on the time of year and how warm (or cold) your kitchen gets. My visual cues are simple: double in size for the first proof and expand to fill the loaf pans for the second. Finally, fill 'em up however you want! These recipes are fun takes on ways you can step up your babka game, but with this master dough, the combinations are truly endless.

You Can Go Your Own Way:
Babka Edition

YIELD: MAKES 2 LOAVES

PREP TIME: 40 MINUTES, PLUS 1 HOUR 45 MINUTES PROOFING TIME

COOK TIME: 40 MINUTES

1 cup whole milk, heated to 115°F

⅓ cup (67g) sugar

1 (¼-ounce) packet active dry yeast (2¼ teaspoons)

4 ounces (1 stick) unsalted butter, melted

4 large eggs

5 cups (675g) all-purpose flour, plus more for dusting

2 teaspoons kosher salt

4 tablespoons vegetable oil

1 recipe babka filling (recipes follow)

1 In the bowl of a stand mixer fitted with the whisk attachment, whisk the warm milk and sugar together. Sprinkle the yeast over the top and let stand until foamy, 5 to 10 minutes.

2 Add the melted butter and 3 of the eggs, then whisk until well incorporated. Switch to the dough hook, then add the flour and salt. Beginning on low speed and gradually increasing to medium, knead until a smooth, elastic dough forms, about 5 minutes.

3 Grease a medium bowl and your hands with 2 tablespoons of the oil. Using your hands, transfer the dough to the bowl, gently turning to coat it with the oil, and shape it into a smooth ball. Cover with plastic wrap or a clean kitchen towel and set aside in a warm place until doubled in size, 1 hour to 1 hour 30 minutes. (Alternatively, you

can let the dough rise in the refrigerator, covered, overnight.)

4 Preheat the oven to 350°F. Grease two 9 by 5-inch loaf pans with the remaining oil, using 1 tablespoon for each pan.

5 Divide the dough into 2 equal balls. On a lightly floured surface, roll out one ball of dough into a 12 by 14-inch rectangle, about ¼ inch thick and aligned horizontally.

6 Spread half the filling evenly over the surface of the dough, leaving a 1-inch border all the way around the rectangle. Starting with the edge closest to you, roll up the dough tightly into a log. Using a serrated knife, carefully cut the roll lengthwise in half. Twist the strands together and pinch the ends to seal. (See photos.)

Carefully place the babka in one of the prepared loaf pans.

7 Repeat this process with the remaining dough and filling. Cover both babkas loosely with plastic wrap or clean kitchen towels and set aside in a warm area until the dough expands to fill the pan, about 45 minutes.

8 In a small bowl, beat the remaining egg, then liberally brush each babka with the egg. Bake, rotating the pans halfway through, for 35 to 40 minutes, until the babkas are golden and each has reached an internal temperature of 185°F.

9 Remove from the oven and let cool slightly in the pans, then remove the loaves from the pans and let cool completely before slicing and serving. Babka is best served the day it's baked.

▌ **Make It Parve!** If you're looking to keep the dough parve, substitute 1 cup water for the milk and substitute ½ cup vegetable oil for the butter.

▌ **Twist and Shout!** While I swear by the slice-and-twist method I use in my recipe, this is not the only way you can twist up your babka. The first variation I learned from Jared Plaxe, a former classmate who was working at Sadelle's in NYC, baking up babka on the daily under Melissa Weller's incredible bread program. After you roll each piece of dough

into a log, instead of slicing it lengthwise, slice it crosswise for two equal-size rolls. Use your hands to gently stretch each slightly, then twist the two together and place in the prepared pan.

Then, of course, there is the method preferred by the equally iconic and Jewish Melissa, Melissa Clark. I absolutely adore her double twist, where you slice lengthwise and twist like I do, but then bring the two ends of the twist together to fold and then twist them again! If that didn't make any sense, just go watch the video of her making it for NYT Cooking.

Chocolate-Tahini Babka Filling

1 cup dark chocolate chips
4 ounces (1 stick) unsalted butter
¼ cup (50g) granulated sugar
1 teaspoon kosher salt
¼ cup tahini
2 tablespoons white sesame seeds, for garnish

Place the chocolate in a heatproof medium bowl.

In a medium saucepan, melt the butter over medium-high heat. Cook, stirring continuously, until browned and nutty in aroma, 6 to 8 minutes. Pour the melted butter over the chocolate, then add the sugar, salt, and tahini. Whisk until a smooth ganache forms, then let cool to room temperature.

Fill the babka dough as directed on page 182 and garnish the babkas with the sesame seeds right before baking.

Babka French Toast! Like most breads, babka is best served the same day it is baked. However, day-old babka lends itself to a transformative journey into some the best French toast you've ever had. Slice up any leftovers into 1-inch-thick slices, then soak them for 5 minutes in a batter of 2 cups whole milk, 2 tablespoons sugar, ½ teaspoon kosher salt, and 3 large eggs (the soaked babka will be delicate, so gently remove the slices from the egg mixture with a spatula). Heat a dab of unsalted butter in a nonstick skillet over medium heat and cook, working in batches and flipping the slices once, until golden and cooked through, 2 to 3 minutes per side. Divide among plates and serve with maple syrup!

Pumpkin Spice Babka Filling

1½ cups canned pumpkin puree
½ cup packed (100g) dark brown sugar
2 teaspoons ground cinnamon
1 teaspoon kosher salt
1 teaspoon ground ginger
1 teaspoon freshly grated nutmeg
¼ teaspoon ground cloves
¼ teaspoon ground allspice
¼ cup maple syrup, for brushing

In a medium bowl, whisk together the pumpkin puree, brown sugar, cinnamon, salt, ginger, nutmeg, cloves, and allspice until smooth.

Fill and bake the babka dough as directed on page 182. Brush the babkas with the maple syrup as soon as they come out of the oven.

Reuben Babka Filling

12 ounces thick-cut pastrami, finely chopped

8 ounces Swiss cheese, coarsely grated

1 cup sauerkraut, drained

½ cup mayonnaise

¼ cup ketchup

1 tablespoon Dijon mustard

1 tablespoon caraway seeds, for garnish

In a medium bowl, stir together the pastrami, cheese, sauerkraut, mayonnaise, ketchup, and mustard until well combined.

Fill the babka dough as directed on page 182 and garnish the babkas with the caraway seeds right before baking.

Ready for an *Inception*-level meltdown? Slice it up and use it to make . . . well another Reuben!

Pistachio Pesto and Sun-Dried Tomato Babka Filling

2 cups packed fresh basil leaves

1 cup finely grated Parmesan cheese

½ cup shelled pistachios

⅓ cup extra-virgin olive oil

2 garlic cloves, smashed and peeled

Grated zest and juice of 1 lemon

Kosher salt

¾ cup sun-dried tomatoes in oil, drained and finely chopped

In a food processor, combine the basil, ½ cup of the Parmesan, the pistachios, olive oil, garlic, and lemon zest and juice. Puree until smooth, then season with salt. Transfer to a bowl and stir in the remaining ½ cup Parmesan and the sun-dried tomatoes.

Fill and bake the babka dough as directed on page 182.

Screw sourdough—slice up this loaf and use it for your next grilled cheese!

Rugelach'ed out of Heaven

Everyone has that one sweet from their childhood that bubbles up all those fuzzy, nostalgic vibes. For me, it's rugelach, those flaky crescents of cream cheese dough rolled up with anything from chocolate to jam to nuts. Every year as far back as I can remember, Evelyn Offner, a dear family friend, would drop off a giant aluminum tray packed with dozens of rugelach for my family right before Rosh Hashanah, and all hell would break loose. In a scene reminiscent of a Walmart on Black Friday, my mother, sister, and I would fight like animals to grab as many of her dark chocolate or cinnamon-walnut rolled beauties as we could. And they almost certainly never lasted long enough to make it to the Jewish New Year.

After years of asking, Evelyn was gracious enough to share her recipe with me, and I've since adapted it with every possible filling combination you can imagine. These four variations are my favorites, spanning both sweet and savory, so you're ready for any occasion!

For those looking to veer toward a sweet to nosh on with coffee, upgrade the classic chocolate filling with chocolate-hazelnut spread and adorn it with crumbles of halva for the gorgeous pairing of chocolate and sesame. For jelly lovers, throw on some peanut butter, packing the ultimate sandwich into the ultimate cookie.

If you're ready to embrace rugelach as the buttery, poppable party app I'm trying to rebrand it as, let's talk. Since it's already a cream cheese dough, you can schmear it with a little more, laced with chopped scallions and lox, of course, for all the flavors of your morning bagel, including the everything bagel seasoning. To finish off this Jewish quartet, cacio e pepe rugelach need no further explanation than that they're cheesy bites of heaven and I will typically eat a dozen in one sitting.

Whichever route you take, I promise it couldn't be any simpler—the dough comes together in minutes and the filling combinations require, at most, one bowl for stirring. Let's get rolling.

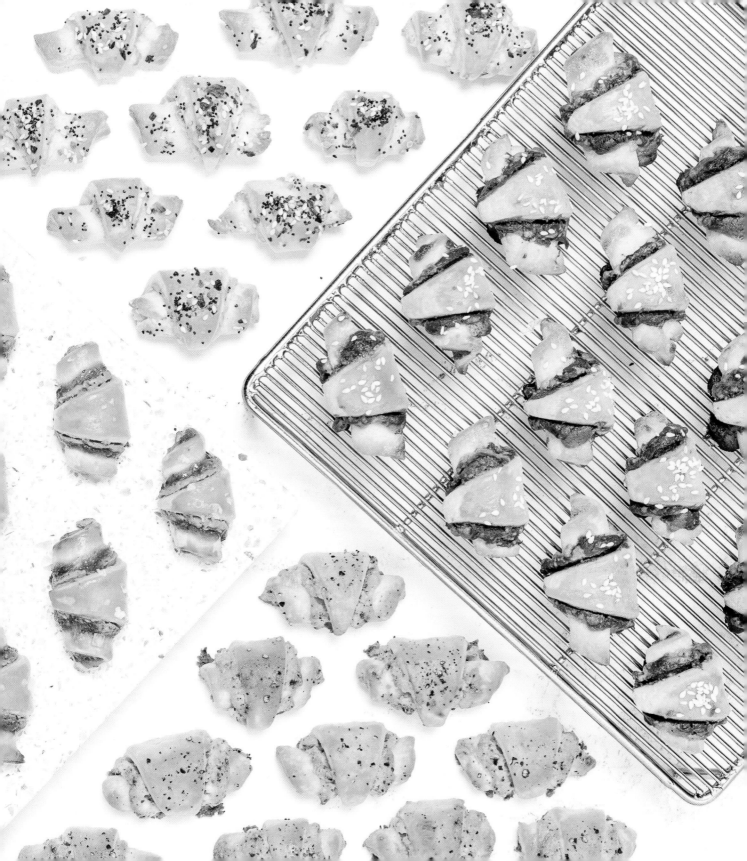

You Can Go Your Own Way:
Rugelach Edition

YIELD: MAKES 48 RUGELACH

PREP TIME: 30 MINUTES, PLUS 1 HOUR CHILLING TIME

COOK TIME: 20 MINUTES

8 ounces cream cheese, at room temperature

4 ounces (1 stick) unsalted butter, at room temperature

¼ cup confectioners' sugar

2⅓ cups (315g) all-purpose flour, plus more for dusting

½ teaspoon kosher salt

1 recipe rugelach filling (recipes follow)

1 large egg, beaten

1 In the bowl of a stand mixer fitted with the paddle attachment, combine the cream cheese, butter, and confectioners' sugar. Beginning on low speed and gradually increasing to medium, mix until light and fluffy, about 2 minutes. Add the flour and salt, then mix until a smooth dough forms. Divide the dough into 4 equal disks, wrap each in plastic wrap, and refrigerate for 1 hour.

2 Preheat the oven to 375°F. Line two half sheet pans with parchment paper.

3 On a lightly floured work surface, roll out one disk of the dough into a 9-inch round. Spread one-quarter of the filling evenly over the dough, leaving a ½-inch border. Slice the dough into 12 even wedges. Roll each wedge up tightly from the outside edge in, then place the rugelach on one of the prepared sheet pans, spacing them ½ inch apart. Repeat with the remaining dough and filling, dividing the rugelach between the prepared pans. Brush the rugelach with the beaten egg.

4 Bake, rotating the pans halfway through, for 20 to 22 minutes, until the rugelach are golden brown. Let cool slightly, then serve.

PB&J Rugelach Filling

¾ cup smooth peanut butter, at room temperature

¾ cup jam or jelly of your choosing

Flaky sea salt, for garnish

Spread 3 tablespoons of the peanut butter over each disk of dough, then spread 3 tablespoons of the jam or jelly on top. Garnish each rugelach with a pinch of flaky sea salt before baking.

Everything Bagel Rugelach Filling

8 ounces cream cheese, at room temperature

4 ounces Nova smoked salmon, finely chopped

1 scallion, thinly sliced

Kosher salt

Everything Seasoning (page 9), for garnish

In a small bowl, mix together the cream cheese, smoked salmon, and scallion until smooth, then season with salt. Garnish each rugelach with a pinch of everything bagel seasoning before baking.

Cacio e Pepe Rugelach Filling

2 cups freshly and finely grated Parmesan cheese

2 cups freshly and finely grated Pecorino Romano cheese

½ cup mayonnaise

1 tablespoon freshly ground black pepper, plus more for garnish

In a small bowl, mix together the Parmesan, Pecorino, mayonnaise, and pepper until smooth. Garnish each rugelach with a pinch of pepper before baking.

Nutella-Halva Rugelach Filling

1 cup Nutella chocolate-hazelnut spread

¾ cup halva crumbles

White sesame seeds, for garnish

Spread ¼ cup of the Nutella over each disk of dough and top with 3 tablespoons of the halva crumbles. Garnish each rugelach with a pinch of sesame seeds before baking.

passover

This menu is too good to pass over! I'll see myself out.

For the Seder Plate

Skip the appetizers and give all your guests a modern seder plate that they can nosh on while you read the four questions.

Smoky Deviled Eggs (page 69)

Typically a roasted egg, the *beitzah* represents the festival sacrifices and the circle of life.

Pomegranate-BBQ Chicken Wings (page 61)

Typically a lamb shank, the *zeroa* represents the lamb sacrificed by the Israelites right before leaving Egypt.

Horseradish Mayo (page 8)

Typically fresh horseradish, the *maror* offers a taste of the bitterness of slavery. Schmear some horseradish mayo on a piece of matzo for each guest.

Walnuts and Date Syrup

Depending on where you're from, the sweet fruit and/or nut paste known as *charoset* could take many forms, though always symbolizing the forced labor of the Israelite slaves to build with brick and mortar. The Iraqi version uses chopped walnuts (I keep mine whole) sweetened with date syrup.

Little Gem Salad with Pickled Celery and Tahini Dressing (page 83)

Typically, romaine lettuce serves as *hazeret*, the second bitter herb on the plate, reinforcing the taste of the bitterness the Jews faced. A mini wedge of dressed-up Little Gem does the trick, too.

Kale Tabbouleh Salad (page 91)

Usually parsley dipped in salt water, *karpas* represents both springtime and the harsh conditions the slaves faced in Egypt. Instead, I serve a scoop of my Kale Tabbouleh, which has a healthy sprinkle of chopped parsley and salt mixed in. Feel free to swap in snap peas for the apples and sautéed asparagus for the butternut squash to make it more spring forward.

Orange Segments

A modern addition to my seder plate, orange segments represent solidarity with LGBTQ+ Jews and others marginalized within the Jewish community. Everyone gets a segment, spitting out the seeds, which symbolize homophobia.

For Dinner

Salted Honey Chopped Liver (page 73)

Roasted Chicken Matzo Ball Soup (page 147)

Roasted Tomato Brisket (page 156)

Sautéed Asparagus with Apricot and Lemon (page 112)

Brown Butter–Rosemary Mashed Potatoes (page 111)

For Dessert

Macaroon Brownies (page 199)

Tiramatzu (Matzo Tiramisu, page 207)

Lotte's Meringue Cookies (page 214)

Flourless Almond Layer Cake with Chocolate Buttercream (page 201)

Rainbow Cookies (page 210)

desserts

Macaroon Brownies

YIELD: MAKES 24 BROWNIES

PREP TIME: 20 MINUTES, PLUS 1 HOUR CHILLING TIME

COOK TIME: 35 MINUTES

If you can believe it, brownies are actually the food I hold closest to my Jewish identity. It all began with the tragic shooting in 2018 at the Tree of Life synagogue in Pittsburgh, the deadliest act of anti-Semitism ever to occur in North America. It took place the morning of our final wedding celebration in Los Angeles. While the party was beautiful, it was extremely difficult to know that as one Jewish family gathered to celebrate such a joyous occasion, others had just begun to sit shiva for loved ones lost that very morning in such an unacceptable act of hate.

OneTable, the Shabbat-focused nonprofit I work with, called for solidarity Shabbats across the country so Jews could gather not to only mourn, but to openly celebrate Jewish ritual and connect with their community in a time of need. Alex and I had just returned to New York on a red-eye that Monday morning, and I so vividly remember turning to him as we waited to exit the plane to express that we had to host Shabbat that Friday.

I had no idea when I'd find time to prep or if anyone would even come—I just knew this was no longer a posh dinner party, but a community forum. Attending simply meant increasing the visibility of Jewish culture while aligning ourselves with this marginalized group that needed to see and feel support. Celebrating Shabbat in that moment was an immediate way to organize and stand up against hate.

I asked everyone who had been to one of my previous Shabbats to come, and even posted an open invitation on Instagram to truly anyone in need of a place to celebrate. My intimate twelve-person rendezvous turned into a fifty-person gathering in the lounge of my building where I served brisket and *tahdig* and kugel and . . . brownies. In order to feed the crowd, with a few adjustments I scaled up my brownie recipe to fill an entire half sheet pan. The resulting squares of fudgy heaven were better than any I had ever made before. In a truly poetic form of Jewish hospitality, it turned out that the secret to my brownie recipe was making enough to share with all. They've become so integral to my Shabbat practice that people ask if I'm making them the second they receive an invitation.

While my sheet pan brownies are the only secret recipe I keep, I had to include them in some form in this book. This is an even more Jewish adaptation of them, turned into a K4P (or kosher for Passover for the abbreviation-adverse) creation Frankensteined with a classic coconut macaroon. A rich ganache-based batter is held together with coconut flour and topped with an equally thick layer of meringue-bound shredded coconut. It's the closest thing you'll get to my coveted brownie recipe, so savor every bite!

RECIPE CONTINUES

8 ounces dark chocolate (70 percent cacao), coarsely chopped

8 ounces (2 sticks) unsalted butter, or 1 cup coconut oil

4 large eggs

1 cup (200g) granulated sugar

¼ cup packed (50g) light brown sugar

2 tablespoons unsweetened cocoa powder

1 tablespoon vanilla extract

1 teaspoon kosher salt

1 teaspoon instant espresso powder

1 cup coconut flour

1 cup milk chocolate chips

FOR THE MACAROON LAYER

4 large egg whites

¾ cup (150g) granulated sugar

1½ teaspoons vanilla extract

½ teaspoon kosher salt

4 cups unsweetened finely shredded coconut (12 ounces)

1 For the brownie layer: Line a 9 by 13-inch baking pan with parchment paper, leaving overhang on all sides.

2 Set a medium metal bowl over a small pot of simmering water. Put the dark chocolate and butter in the bowl and heat, stirring occasionally, until completely melted and combined, then remove from the heat.

3 Meanwhile, in a large bowl, whisk together the eggs, granulated sugar, brown sugar, cocoa powder, vanilla, salt, and espresso powder until smooth. Whisk in the melted chocolate mixture until smooth. Fold in the coconut flour until just incorporated, followed by the milk chocolate chips. Scrape the batter into the prepared pan and spread it into an even layer. Refrigerate for 1 hour.

4 For the macaroon layer: Preheat the oven to 375°F.

5 In the bowl of a stand mixer fitted with the whisk attachment, whisk the egg whites on medium speed until frothy, then, with the mixer running, slowly add the granulated sugar, vanilla, and salt. Whisk, gradually increasing the speed to high, until the egg whites hold stiff peaks. Add the coconut and mix on low speed until just incorporated. Spread the coconut mixture into an even layer over the chilled brownie layer.

6 Bake for about 30 minutes, until just set and the coconut is golden. Let cool completely. Remove from the pan, slice into 24 brownies, and serve.

Note: These brownies are best served the same day they're baked. Store any leftovers in an airtight container at room temperature and serve within three days for peak enjoyment.

The more I bake brownies for others, the more I realize how divided the world is between those who crave dense, fudgy brownies and those who crave tender, cakey brownies. While this recipe is that perfect balance of the two, I have a hack for those on the hunt for extra-fudgy squares. Reduce the coconut flour to ¾ cup and discover borderline brownie-batter bliss.

Flourless Almond Layer Cake
with Chocolate Buttercream

YIELD: SERVES 10 TO 12

PREP TIME: 30 MINUTES, PLUS COOLING TIME

COOK TIME: 30 MINUTES

Honestly, the Passover desserts in this book are some of my favorites. This one in particular is dedicated to Enid Fisher, our sister-in-law's mother. Enid's birthday often falls on or around the Passover seders, so it's become a yearly tradition that I make this flourless almond layer cake for seder dessert. That way, we don't have to stick the candles in the fruit salad. It truly is treated just like a typical yellow cake with chocolate buttercream, but just so happens to be completely gluten-free, so while you're sulking over that dry flourless chocolate cake your aunt brought, we're going wild with this three-tier sensation.

Using meringue to leaven and a ridiculous amount of butter for flavor, it's honestly a great cake for any time of year, especially for a birthday party. Typically when you make a layer cake, you pretty much have to assemble it the day you serve it, and the second it goes into the fridge, it dries out. I'm sorry, but if I'm hosting or cooking, that just doesn't fit my schedule. Since this is almond-flour based, the cake stays just as moist when refrigerated from the night before, and dare I say it might even taste better. That carries on to the leftovers (if you have any), which will keep in the fridge for days of late-night sweet-tooth binges.

Feel free to decorate as you please! I've done everything from macaron shell polka dots to fresh fruit dusted with confectioners' sugar to just a ridiculous amount of rainbow sprinkles. Any way you slice it, you're going to change your seder dessert game forever.

RECIPE CONTINUES

12 ounces (3 sticks) unsalted butter, at room temperature, plus more for greasing

5¼ cups (500g) finely ground almond flour

3 cups (250g) confectioners' sugar

2 teaspoons kosher salt

12 large eggs, separated

2 tablespoons granulated sugar

FOR THE FROSTING

1 cup milk chocolate chips

1 cup dark chocolate chips

½ cup full-fat sour cream

1 pound (4 sticks) unsalted butter, at room temperature

1 cup confectioners' sugar

1 teaspoon vanilla extract

½ teaspoon kosher salt

1 For the almond cakes: Preheat the oven to 350°F. Grease three 8-inch round cake pans with butter and line with parchment paper cut to fit.

2 In the bowl of a stand mixer fitted with the paddle attachment, combine the butter, almond flour, confectioners' sugar, and salt. Beginning on low speed and gradually increasing to medium, mix until a smooth paste forms. Add the egg yolks and mix until smooth, then transfer the batter to a large bowl. Clean the stand mixer bowl and return it to the mixer.

3 Switch to the whisk attachment. Put the egg whites and granulated sugar in the clean stand mixer bowl and whisk on medium-high speed until the egg whites hold stiff peaks. Gently fold the whipped egg whites into the batter until just incorporated. Divide the batter evenly among the prepared cake pans, smoothing the tops with a rubber or offset spatula.

4 Bake for 25 to 30 minutes, until the cakes are risen and golden, with no jiggle when you gently shake the pans. Let cool completely, then run a paring knife around the side of each cake and invert them onto wire racks lined with parchment. Remove the pans and discard the parchment rounds from baking.

5 For the frosting: While the cakes cool, set a medium metal bowl over a small pot of simmering water. Put the milk and dark chocolate chips in the bowl and heat, stirring occasionally, until completely melted and combined. Remove from the heat and whisk in the sour cream until smooth. Let cool to room temperature.

6 In the bowl of a stand mixer fitted with the paddle attachment, combine the butter and confectioners' sugar. Beginning on low speed and gradually increasing to medium, beat until light and fluffy, 2 to 3 minutes. Add the cooled melted chocolate mixture, the vanilla, and the salt, then mix until smooth, 1 to 2 minutes.

7 To assemble, carefully place one of the cooled cakes on a cake stand, then, using an offset spatula, spread 1 cup of the frosting over the top of the cake in an even layer. Carefully set another cake on top of the first and spread 1 cup of the frosting over the top of the cake in an even layer. Carefully set the remaining cake on top of the second and spread 1 cup of the frosting over the top of the cake in an even layer. Spread the remaining frosting over the sides of the cake to cover it completely, using a large offset spatula or bench scraper to smooth the edges. Let stand at room temperature for 20 minutes, then slice and serve.

Sour Cherry
Rice Pudding

YIELD: SERVES 6 TO 8

PREP TIME: 15 MINUTES, PLUS COOLING TIME

COOK TIME: 55 MINUTES

Many kids got their sugar high from Jell-O or choco-late pudding cups, but for as long as I can remember, I've had an affinity for rice pudding cups. Like many octogenarian-acting children, I adored gumming down on the chewy texture rice adds to a silky pudding while imparting the subtle flavor of the rice into the mix. This Persian version was dreamt up while I was preparing a pot of *albaloo polo,* Alex's favorite variation of Persian rice. Laced with stewed sour cherries, it's a side dish that skews on the sweet side. With the same innovation that brought you savory kugel (see page 129), today, I push all boundaries and make *albaloo polo* a dessert. By topping a fragrant basmati rice pudding with spiced sour cherry compote, you get all the same flavors, layered in a comforting bowl and served up warm—though it's also great chilled, depending on your fancy.

If you've never played around with sour cherries in your all-American cherry pie, you're missing out on one of summer's most vibrant gems. Offering the perfect level of tart-ness, tamed with just a touch of sugar, they're well worth the time you'll spend pitting them. In this compote, I pair them with warm spices like cinnamon and cardamom, as well as the almighty black peppercorn, which you'll grow to see is a match made in heaven with cherries and berries alike. And if you're as forward-thinking as I am when it comes to a sugar craving, stock up on sour cherries while they're in season. You can pit a huge batch to store in the freezer, arming yourself to whip up this compote any time of year. Though I give you my blessing to pivot to fresh sweet cherries if you're really in a crunch.

RECIPE CONTINUES

2 cups pitted fresh sour cherries

¼ cup sugar

1 teaspoon ground cinnamon

½ teaspoon ground coriander

½ teaspoon kosher salt

¼ teaspoon ground cardamom

Pinch of freshly ground black pepper

2 tablespoons cornstarch

FOR THE RICE PUDDING

5 whole green cardamom pods, smashed

1 (4-inch) cinnamon stick

4 cups whole milk

1 cup uncooked basmati rice

⅓ cup sugar

1 teaspoon kosher salt

2 tablespoons cornstarch

Chopped pistachios, for garnish

1 For the compote: In a medium saucepan, combine the cherries, sugar, cinnamon, coriander, salt, ground cardamom, and pepper. Cook over medium heat, stirring often, until the cherries are tender and in a pool of their juices, 12 to 15 minutes.

2 In a small bowl, stir together the cornstarch and 2 tablespoons cool water until smooth, then add the mixture to the pot with the cherries. Simmer, stirring often, until thickened, 3 to 4 minutes more. Transfer the cherry compote to a bowl and let cool.

3 For the rice pudding: In a medium saucepan, toast the cardamom pods and cinnamon stick over medium heat until fragrant, about 1 minute. Pour in the milk and 2 cups water and bring to a simmer. Add the rice, sugar, and salt and bring to a light simmer. Cook, stirring occasionally, until the rice is very tender, about 30 minutes.

4 In a small bowl, stir together the cornstarch and 2 tablespoons cool water until smooth, then stir the mixture into the rice. Simmer the rice pudding until thickened, 4 to 5 minutes more. Remove from the heat and let cool slightly. Discard the cardamom pods and cinnamon stick.

5 Divide the rice pudding among serving bowls and spoon over the sour cherry compote. Garnish with chopped pistachios, then serve.

Tiramatzu (Matzo Tiramisu)

YIELD: SERVES 8 TO 10

PREP TIME: 30 MINUTES, PLUS 4 HOURS CHILLING TIME

COOK TIME: 10 MINUTES

6 large egg yolks

½ cup plus 2 tablespoons (125g) granulated sugar

¼ cup plus 2 tablespoons Kahlúa or other coffee liqueur

1 teaspoon vanilla extract

1 teaspoon kosher salt

1½ cups heavy cream

1 cup mascarpone, at room temperature

1¼ cups hot coffee

6 sheets matzo

2 tablespoons unsweetened cocoa powder, for garnish

I'd love to take credit for thinking of this idea, but I didn't. Julie Resnick, cofounder of Feedfeed, saw a matzo icebox cake I posted on my Instagram a few years ago and thought to do a tiramisu-inspired version for Pesach. Pure genius! Think about it: matzo is just as dry as ladyfingers, so why not make one swap and be set with your Passover dessert? While her kids call her creation *matzomasu*, I've stepped in with my own punny variation—it's known in my house as *tiramatzu*. In my recipe, a creamy mixture of zabaglione and whipped cream is layered between coffee-soaked sheets of matzo for probably the most decadent dessert in this entire book.

If you've never made zabaglione (known as sabayon in French) before, it's the king of custards. Though it's traditionally made with sweet wine, I sub in coffee liqueur and whisk it with egg yolks and sugar over a double boiler until the mixture has thickened and tripled in volume. To make the zabaglione even richer, I fold in whipped cream and mascarpone before layering it with the matzo to achieve a hint of lightness in such a rich sweet. The dish needs to set up in the fridge to let the matzo soften, so it lends itself well to being made a day in advance of seder, and only requires a dusting of cocoa powder before you scoop in.

1 Set a large metal bowl over a medium pot of simmering water. In the bowl, combine the egg yolks, ½ cup of the sugar, 2 tablespoons of the Kahlúa, the vanilla, and the salt. Heat, whisking continuously, until the mixture is pale yellow, thickened, and tripled in volume, 6 to 8 minutes. Remove from the heat.

2 In another large bowl, using a handheld mixer, whip the heavy cream to stiff peaks. Gently fold the whipped cream and mascarpone into the egg mixture.

3 In a shallow baking dish or quarter sheet pan, stir together the hot coffee, remaining 2 tablespoons sugar, and remaining ¼ cup Kahlúa until the sugar has dissolved.

4 To assemble, soak 1 sheet of matzo in the hot coffee mixture for 30 seconds. Place the soaked matzo on the bottom of a 2-quart casserole dish or 9-inch square baking dish, breaking it into pieces to fit if needed. Spread 1 cup of the cream mixture evenly over the matzo. Repeat this process of soaking and layering until all the matzo and cream mixture have been used. Cover and refrigerate for at least 4 hours or preferably overnight before serving.

5 Using a fine-mesh sieve, dust the cocoa powder over the tiramatzu right before scooping and serving.

Rainbow Cookies

YIELD: MAKES 35 COOKIES

PREP TIME: 30 MINUTES, PLUS COOLING
AND 1 HOUR CHILLING TIME

COOK TIME: 15 MINUTES

10 ounces (2½ sticks) unsalted butter, at room temperature, plus more for greasing

4⅓ cups (410g) finely ground almond flour

2½ cups (205g) confectioners' sugar

1½ teaspoons kosher salt

2 teaspoons almond extract

10 large eggs, separated

1 to 2 teaspoons green food coloring

1 to 2 teaspoons red food coloring

½ cup raspberry jam or apricot preserves

½ cup Nutella chocolate-hazelnut spread or tahini

1½ cups semisweet chocolate chips

2 tablespoons coconut oil

If I'm going to taste the rainbow, it's always going to be double-fisting rainbow cookies until I'm sick. Growing up, someone would always bring a plastic container of fluorescent store-bought rainbow cookies to any and every holiday, and it was always the first dessert to go. My obsession carried into adulthood, as I found a man who insists on stopping into bakeries to buy exactly two rainbow cookies to snack on no matter what time of day it is.

In my version, layers of tender almond cake are sandwiched with fillings of your choosing and schmeared with chocolate for sandwich-cookie heaven. And while I don't use almond paste in the batter, I exclusively use almond flour, resulting in a not-intentionally gluten-free and kosher-for-Passover confection. Since we're going the almond flour route, a hefty meringue is required to give the layers the lift they need. When you're incorporating the whipped egg whites into the batter, work in batches to ensure they are evenly incorporated and you don't end up with lumps, or the cakes won't bake evenly.

Let's chat fillings. While I used to use a single filling for the whole cake, I've fallen in love with mixing and matching to combine flavors that truly pop. Try using apricot preserves for one layer and tahini for the other, or raspberry jam and Nutella. You can pick whatever combo you'd like! I'm going to let you be as simple or creative as you want with this one—just aim for ½ cup of something sweet between each layer.

1 Preheat the oven to 350°F. Grease three quarter sheet pans with butter and line them with parchment paper.

2 In a medium bowl, whisk together the almond flour, confectioners' sugar, and salt until combined.

3 In the bowl of a stand mixer fitted with the paddle attachment, beat the butter and almond extract on medium speed for 2 minutes, until light and fluffy. Add the egg yolks one at a time, mixing well after each addition. With the motor running, slowly add the dry ingredients and mix until incorporated, then transfer the batter to a large bowl. Clean the stand mixer bowl and return it to the mixer.

4 Switch to the whisk attachment. Put the egg whites in the clean stand mixer bowl and whisk on medium-high speed until they hold stiff peaks, then gently fold them into the batter in three additions. Divide the batter among three bowls. Stir the green food coloring into one bowl and the red food coloring into another. Leave the third bowl untinted.

5 Spread the batter from each bowl evenly into the prepared pans. Bake until risen and firm, about 15 minutes. Let the layers cool completely, then run a paring knife around the sides of each layer and invert them onto a cutting board. Remove the pans and discard the parchment paper.

6 Line one of the quarter sheet pans with clean parchment, then place

the red layer on it. Spread the fruit preserves evenly over the red layer, then place the white layer on top and spread the Nutella over it. Top with the green layer.

7 In a small microwave-safe bowl, combine the chocolate chips and the coconut oil. Microwave in 30-second intervals, stirring after each, until melted and smooth. Spread half the chocolate mixture evenly over the rainbow cookies and refrigerate until firm, 30 minutes.

8 Carefully flip the cookies and spread the remaining chocolate mixture evenly over the bare side. Refrigerate until firm, for 30 minutes.

9 Transfer to a cutting board and trim the edges. Cut into 1½-inch squares, then transfer to a platter and serve.

Chewy Iraqi Almond Cookies
(Hadji Bada)

YIELD: MAKES 24 COOKIES

PREP TIME: 20 MINUTES, PLUS
COOLING TIME

COOK TIME: 15 MINUTES

2 cups finely ground almond flour

½ teaspoon ground cinnamon

½ teaspoon kosher salt

2 large egg whites

1 cup (200g) sugar

1 tablespoon rose water, plus more for rolling

24 whole raw almonds

A few years into dating, Alex and I combined families for Passover seder, where I cooked a feast with his aunt Diana, spanning all the staple dishes from both the Ashkenazi and Mizrahi sides—minus gefilte fish, much to my mother's chagrin. Our Manischewitz-stained apple *charoset* sat next to their *charoset* of date syrup and crushed walnuts. Platters of braised brisket alternated with beet *kubbeh* and *tahdig*. It was the ultimate blending of cultures, fusing our families and traditions. But the highlight of the evening for me was the arrival of Alex's ninety-something-year-old great-aunt Doris, who I had yet to meet. She entered the dining room holding a folded piece of paper for me with her recipe for *hadji bada*, Iraqi almond cookies, scribbled on it, knowing I was on the hunt to learn family recipes to make for Alex.

It's the gift that keeps on giving, since this recipe has become a staple sweet for any occasion. Likened to French macarons without the meringue, they sport a combo of almond flour, egg whites, rose water, and sugar that bakes into chewy clouds of floral sweetness. To add a little pizzazz, I threw in some cinnamon to give warm snickerdoodle vibes when paired with almond. Adorned with a single almond on top, they're as easy to make as they are to eat—plus, they just so happen to be gluten-free.

1 Preheat the oven to 350°F. Line two half sheet pans with parchment paper.

2 In a medium bowl, whisk together the almond flour, cinnamon, and salt to combine.

3 In a large bowl, whisk the egg whites, sugar, and rose water until foamy. (Note: You're not making a meringue.) Stir in the almond flour mixture until a smooth dough forms.

4 Fill a small bowl with room-temperature water and add a few drops of rose water, then use this water to wet your hands to prevent sticking as you roll the dough. Roll the dough into tablespoon-size balls and place them on the prepared sheet pans, spacing them 2 inches apart and placing 12 balls on each pan. Push an almond into the center of each ball of dough.

5 Bake, rotating the pans halfway through, for about 15 minutes, until the cookies have spread out and their edges are golden. Let cool completely on the pans, then serve.

Lotte's Meringue Cookies

YIELD: MAKES ABOUT 36 COOKIES

PREP TIME: 20 MINUTES, PLUS
COOLING TIME

COOK TIME: 2 HOURS 5 MINUTES

3 large egg whites

¼ teaspoon cream of tartar

1 cup (200g) sugar

2 teaspoons cornstarch

1 teaspoon kosher salt

1 teaspoon vanilla extract

5 ounces dark chocolate (70 percent cacao), chopped (1 cup)

1 cup walnuts, coarsely chopped

While I never met my great-grandfather, I grew up with his brother's wife, my great-great-aunt Lotte. She celebrated pretty much every holiday with us, arriving each time with a Tupperware of her famous meringue cookies in hand. They were packed with chocolate chips and chopped walnuts, and I was enamored by the way this crisp cookie melted in your mouth the second it touched your tongue. They were my absolute favorite, and she knew it, and she always baked enough so I would have leftovers to snack on for days.

It wasn't until Lotte passed away in 2019 at the grand old age of ninety-seven that my sister and I first learned of her upbringing in Germany. She was our kind, meringue-scooping aunt, but we never knew of her experiences searching for education after being turned away from school for being a Jew, having to wear a yellow Jewish star on her sleeve, escaping to England to work as an underpaid maid, and eventually learning that most of her family had perished in the Holocaust. After so much pain and hardship, Lotte helped build a family full of so much love, one that I'm proud to be a part of.

I've tweaked her meringue recipe over the years, swapping chocolate chips for chopped bar chocolate to add a little more gooeyness and combining her French meringue with a hot cornstarch slurry for extra gloss, a genius technique I learned from my friend and pastry chef extraordinaire Miro Uskokovic of Gramercy Tavern in NYC. But at their core, these will always be Lotte's meringues. And while they may not be inherently Jewish, the story of her perseverance, which eventually led to me having this recipe, brings me more pride as a Jew than any traditional confection, and that is the sweetest part of all.

1 Preheat the oven to 200°F. Line two half sheet pans with parchment paper.

2 In the bowl of a stand mixer fitted with the whisk attachment, whip the egg whites and cream of tartar on medium speed until frothy. Then, with the mixer running, stream in the sugar and whip until white in color and beginning to grow in volume, but not yet able to hold soft peaks.

3 Meanwhile, in a small saucepan, whisk the cornstarch with ⅓ cup water. Cook over medium-high heat, stirring continuously, until thickened, about 2 minutes.

4 With the mixer running, slowly pour the hot cornstarch slurry into the egg white mixture, followed by the salt and vanilla. Raise the mixer speed to medium-high and whip until the mixture holds stiff peaks, 10 to 12 minutes. Gently fold in the chocolate and walnuts.

5 Spoon 2-tablespoon mounds of the meringue mixture onto the prepared sheet pans, spacing them 1 inch

apart. Bake for
2 hours, then remove
from the oven and let
cool completely.

6 Serve once cool, or store
in an airtight container lined
with paper towels at room
temperature for up to 4 days.

Kubaneh Cinnamon Rolls

YIELD: MAKES 8 CINNAMON ROLLS

PREP TIME: 40 MINUTES, PLUS 2 HOURS 15 MINUTES PROOFING TIME

COOK TIME: 45 MINUTES

Yemenite breads are my Jewish kink. You know I'm always going to back up my love for challah, but once you get into the world of laminated carbs from Yemeni Jews, it unlocks a desire to *breadface* any specimen in close proximity. While I could wax poetic about flaky *malawach* or bubbly, chewy *lachuch* all day, let's give all attention to *kubaneh* in today's lesson on these breads. Made from a pull-apart yeast dough, it's baked overnight through the start of Shabbat, ready to tear into on Saturday with spicy Schug (page 11) and grated tomato.

To me, it's as close to Jewish monkey bread as you'll get, so it wasn't so crazy to veer sweet with a cinnamon-and-cardamom-scented filling and a sticky cream cheese glaze. Separate from the fact that we should be constantly striving to put the spotlight on lesser-known Jewish dishes, especially from marginalized communities within the Jewish population, this is simply one of the best cinnamon roll recipes you'll ever tear apart. Instead of making a giant log and slicing it, smaller chunks of dough are rolled up with the filling, then spiralled into tight rolls and nestled next to each other in the pan.

While I'm not baking these all night long through the Sabbath, you can save the second proof for overnight in the fridge on Friday night if you feel so indulgent as to have them fresh for breakfast Saturday morning. That being said, I've served these rolls at breakfast, lunch, and dinner and they've never failed to satisfy any sweet tooth and expand the ever-growing Yemenite bread fan club.

RECIPE CONTINUES

FOR THE DOUGH

1 cup whole milk, heated to 115°F

¼ cup (50g) granulated sugar

1 (¼-ounce) packet active dry yeast (2¼ teaspoons)

4 tablespoons (¾ stick) unsalted butter, melted, plus 2 tablespoons melted butter for brushing

1 large egg

4 cups (540g) all-purpose flour, plus more for dusting

2 teaspoons kosher salt

1 teaspoon baking powder

2 tablespoons vegetable oil, plus 1 tablespoon for the pan

FOR THE FILLING

4 ounces (1 stick) unsalted butter

1 cup packed (200g) dark brown sugar

1 tablespoon ground cinnamon

1 teaspoon ground allspice

1 teaspoon ground cardamom

1 teaspoon kosher salt

FOR THE GLAZE

1½ cups confectioners' sugar

2 tablespoons full-fat cream cheese, at room temperature

2 tablespoons whole milk

½ teaspoon vanilla extract

Pinch of kosher salt

1 For the dough: In the bowl of a stand mixer fitted with the whisk attachment, mix the warm milk and granulated sugar to combine, then sprinkle the yeast over the top. Let stand until foamy, 5 to 10 minutes. Add the 4 tablespoons melted butter and the egg, then whisk on medium speed until incorporated.

2 Switch to the dough hook, then add the flour, salt, and baking powder to the bowl. Beginning on low speed and gradually increasing to medium, knead until a smooth, elastic dough forms, about 5 minutes.

3 Grease a medium bowl and your hands with the 2 tablespoons vegetable oil. Using your hands, transfer the dough to the bowl, gently turning it to coat with the oil, and shape it into a smooth ball. Cover with plastic wrap or a clean kitchen towel and set aside in a warm place until doubled in size, about 1 hour 30 minutes.

4 For the filling: Meanwhile, in a medium saucepan, melt the butter over medium-high heat. Cook, whisking continuously, until golden and nutty in aroma, 6 to 8 minutes. Transfer to a heatproof bowl, then whisk in the brown sugar, cinnamon, allspice, cardamom, and salt until smooth.

5 Grease a 9-inch round cake pan with the 1 tablespoon vegetable oil, then line it with parchment paper cut to fit.

6 Transfer the dough to a lightly floured surface and divide it into 8 equal pieces. Roll one piece of the dough into an 8-inch square. Spread 1½ tablespoons of the filling over the dough, leaving a ½-inch border. Starting with the edge closest to you, tightly roll up the dough into a log, then take one end of the log and spiral it into a tight coil. Place the coiled dough seam-side up in the prepared pan. Repeat the process with the remaining dough and filling, nestling the rolls next to each other in the pan. (See photos.) Cover and set aside in a warm place until puffed to fill out the pan, 45 minutes to 1 hour.

7 Preheat the oven to 350°F.

8 Brush the rolls with the 2 tablespoons melted butter. Bake for 35 to 40 minutes, until golden brown and risen. Remove from the oven and let cool in the pan for 15 minutes.

9 For the glaze: In a medium bowl, whisk together the confectioners' sugar, cream cheese, milk, vanilla, and salt until smooth.

10 Place a plate over the cake pan and invert them together. Remove the pan and discard the parchment. Drizzle the rolls with the glaze, then serve warm.

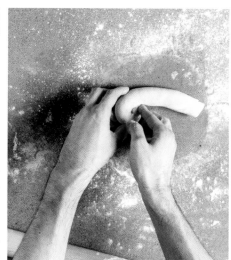

1 Roll one piece of dough into an 8-inch square.

2 Spread 1½ tablespoons of the filling over the dough, leaving a ½-inch border.

3 Tightly roll the dough up into a log.

4 Take one end of the log and spiral it into a tight coil.

5 Place the coil seam-side up in the prepared pan.

Apples and Honey Upside-Down Cake

YIELD: SERVES 10 TO 12

PREP TIME: 20 MINUTES, PLUS
COOLING TIME

COOK TIME: 1 HOUR 10 MINUTES

Nonstick cooking spray, for greasing

3 Honeycrisp apples, cored and sliced
   into 8 wedges each

¾ cup (150g) granulated sugar

8 ounces (2 sticks) unsalted butter

1 cup honey, plus more for garnish
   (optional)

¾ cup buttermilk

2 large eggs

½ cup packed (100g) dark brown sugar

1 teaspoon vanilla extract

2 cups (270g) all-purpose flour

2 teaspoons kosher salt

1 teaspoon ground cinnamon

1 teaspoon freshly grated nutmeg

½ teaspoon baking powder

½ teaspoon baking soda

Whipped cream, for garnish (optional)

There are two reasons to make an upside-down cake. The first is to highlight ripe seasonal fruit by slowly caramelizing it, covered in a cake batter that will soak up all its bubbling juices. The second is that you just cannot be bothered to make a layer cake with the headache of all the cooling, frosting, and decorating. I'll be completely honest: I teeter between the two. While I love the seasonality of alternating among rhubarb, blueberries, peaches, plums, apples, and fall squashes throughout the year, I also love that the whole thing just gets flipped out of one cake pan and I'm done.

Sure, these reasons hold for this apple-studded beauty, but there's a third: I needed a dessert to serve at Rosh Hashanah. To add another layer of Judaism, the apples are topped with a rich honey cake batter to keep with the holiday motif. Served warm, saturated in brown butter and caramel, this dessert will flip anything you knew about honey cake upside down, literally.

1 Preheat the oven to 350°F. Line a high-sided 9-inch round cake pan with parchment paper cut to fit and grease with cooking spray.

2 Line the bottom of the prepared pan with apple wedges, arranging them in concentric circles, then shingle any remaining slices in the center.

3 In a medium saucepan, combine the granulated sugar with 3 tablespoons water. Cook over medium-high heat, shaking the pan as needed, until an amber caramel forms, 6 to 8 minutes.

Immediately pour the caramel over the apples in an even layer.

4 In another medium saucepan, melt the butter over medium heat. Cook, stirring continuously, until browned and nutty in aroma, 6 to 8 minutes. Pour the melted butter into a heatproof large bowl and let cool slightly, then whisk in the honey, buttermilk, eggs, brown sugar, and vanilla until smooth.

5 In a medium bowl, whisk together the flour, salt, cinnamon, nutmeg, baking powder, and baking soda to combine. Add the dry ingredients to

the wet ingredients and fold until just incorporated. Pour the batter over the caramel-coated apples. Bake for 1 hour to 1 hour 10 minutes, until the top is golden and a toothpick inserted into the center comes out clean.

6 Let cool in the pan for 15 minutes, then run a paring knife around the edge of the cake. Place a plate over the cake pan and invert them together, then lift off the pan and remove the parchment. Let the cake cool slightly, then serve warm. Top with whipped cream and drizzle with honey, if desired.

JEW-ISH 220

Plum Crumb Bars

YIELD: SERVES 10 TO 12

PREP TIME: 25 MINUTES, PLUS
COOLING TIME

COOK TIME: 50 MINUTES

FOR THE DOUGH

4 cups (540g) all-purpose flour

1 cup (200g) granulated sugar

⅓ cup raw pistachios

¼ cup packed (50g) light brown sugar

1 teaspoon kosher salt

1 teaspoon baking powder

1 teaspoon ground cinnamon

1 pound (4 sticks) unsalted butter, cubed and chilled

3 large eggs, lightly beaten

FOR THE FILLING

2½ pounds Italian plums (about 12 medium), halved, pitted, and cut into wedges

½ cup (100g) granulated sugar

¼ cup cornstarch

2 tablespoons freshly squeezed lemon juice

½ teaspoon kosher salt

This recipe means the world to me because it is an adaptation of the family recipe that catapulted me into writing about Jewish food. Every Rosh Hashanah, my aunt Susi would make her mother's apple cake, a recipe my Nanny started making in the late 1940s after her family fled Europe for Cuba during the Holocaust. Though she called it a cake, Nanny used a pie dish to push in some of the dough before filling it with apples and pinching off pieces of the remaining dough for a crumb topping. It was half cake, half pie, and all around the best way to start the Jewish New Year on a sweet note.

I finally asked Susi for the recipe a few years ago when I wrote about it for *Saveur*. Within my Nanny's Rolodex of German Jewish recipes, this apple cake was scribbled on an index card, worn out from its lengthy journey to America with my family. While I had tested and adapted hundreds of recipes, this was the first recipe I transcribed to which I had a personal connection. I wasn't just sharing a recipe—I was preserving a little part of Jewish history and offering a piece of my own Jewish narrative.

Writing about apple cake was the first time I felt like I had found my voice as a food writer, which is especially funny here, as there are no apples in this recipe and you're probably extremely confused about how it will all tie together. Since Rosh Hashanah arrives in the beginning of fall, Nanny would often swap out the apples for ripe Italian plums. Over the years, I transformed that equally delectable variation into bars, using the same technique and base dough. There we go. I knew we could land it! With some small additions like pistachios for texture and salt for my sanity, these bars are packed with flavor and Judaism.

1 Preheat the oven to 350°F. Line a 9 by 13-inch baking pan with parchment paper, leaving overhang on all sides.

2 For the dough: In a food processor, pulse the flour, granulated sugar, pistachios, brown sugar, salt, baking powder, and cinnamon to combine. Add the butter and pulse until pea-size crumbles form. Pour in the eggs and pulse until the dough just comes together. Press two-thirds of the dough into the prepared pan in an even layer and set the remainder aside.

3 For the filling: In a medium bowl, toss the plums, granulated sugar, cornstarch, lemon juice, and salt to coat. Pour the plums into the pan and spread them into an even layer. Pinch off small pieces of the remaining dough and scatter them over the plums.

4 Bake for 50 to 55 minutes, until golden brown and bubbling. Let cool in the pan completely, then transfer to a cutting board, slice into squares, and serve.

Note: You can make this recipe a day or two before serving. After cooling, wrap tightly in plastic, and refrigerate until ready to slice and serve. Store any leftovers in an airtight container in the refrigerator for up to one week.

Tahini-Swirled Cheesecake

YIELD: SERVES 8 TO 10

PREP TIME: 30 MINUTES, PLUS OVERNIGHT CHILLING

COOK TIME: 1 HOUR 30 MINUTES

FOR THE CRUST

1½ cups graham cracker crumbs (from about 9 sheets)

4 ounces (1 stick) unsalted butter, cubed

1 teaspoon ground cinnamon

½ teaspoon kosher salt

FOR THE FILLING

4 (8-ounce) packages full-fat cream cheese, at room temperature

1 cup packed (200g) light brown sugar

¾ cup tahini

¼ cup full-fat sour cream

1 teaspoon vanilla extract

1 teaspoon kosher salt

½ teaspoon ground cinnamon

4 large eggs

I grew up making trips to Junior's for cheesecake with my grandmother Marilyn, planting the seeds for my love of dense New York–style cheesecake. That love never faded: When I was working at Daniel, I'd gather friends from culinary school, scattered around the city, at the Junior's in Times Square for communal slices around midnight after our shifts. Luckily, I found myself a man who enjoys cheesecake as much as I do, and who even supports me when I play around with the flavors, like I do in this mash-up of cultures.

A combo of tahini blended into the batter and swirled on top adds richness to the already decadent dessert, and pairing it with a hint of cinnamon amps up the warmth. Wrapped up in a graham cracker crust, it's a fun Middle Eastern spin on a New York classic. But the same cheesecake rules apply! Use a water bath to cook it low and slow before letting it cool completely. Then chill it overnight to ensure it fully sets so you get those super-clean slices. If you're in a time crunch, go wild and break the rules—it will still be delicious.

1 Preheat the oven to 350°F.

2 For the crust: In a food processor, combine the graham cracker crumbs, butter, cinnamon, and salt and pulse until well incorporated. Transfer the crumb mixture to a 9-inch springform pan, pressing it evenly over the bottom and 1 inch up the sides of the pan. Bake for 15 minutes, until golden, then let cool.

3 For the filling: In the bowl of a stand mixer fitted with the paddle attachment, combine the cream cheese, brown sugar, 6 tablespoons of the tahini, the sour cream, vanilla, salt, and cinnamon. Mix on medium speed until smooth. With the mixer running, add the eggs one at a time and mix, stopping to scrape the sides of the bowl as needed, until completely smooth.

4 Wrap the bottom of the cooled springform pan with two large sheets of aluminum foil to completely cover the outside and place in a roasting pan. Pour the cream cheese mixture over the crust. Drizzle the remaining 6 tablespoons tahini over the top and, using a knife, swirl it into the batter.

5 Boil a kettle or small saucepan of water. Place the roasting pan on the middle rack of the oven, then pour boiling water into the roasting pan to come 1 inch up the outside of the foil-wrapped springform pan.

6 Bake for 1 hour 15 minutes, until the cheesecake is just set with only a slight jiggle when gently shaken. Remove the springform pan from the water-filled roasting pan and let cool completely. Cover the cheesecake and refrigerate overnight.

7 The next day, let the cheesecake come to room temperature, then remove the springform ring, slice, and serve.

Salt-and-Pepper Sufganiyot

YIELD: MAKES 15 DOUGHNUTS

PREP TIME: 45 MINUTES, PLUS PROOFING TIME

COOK TIME: 15 MINUTES

I go nuts for doughnuts any time of year, so you can imagine the psychotic break I face every Hanukkah in excitement for *sufganiyot*. And while you don't need a holiday to enjoy a jelly doughnut, these eight crazy nights are when you can eat five in one sitting and nobody judges you. As I've fried up batches over the years, I've slowly crafted a superior dough for these golden pillows. But the true magic comes after frying, when, instead of using the traditional dusting of confectioners' sugar, I toss the freshly fried doughnuts in a mixture of granulated sugar, salt, and black pepper. The punch of salinity helps balance all that sweetness, and the subtle spice of freshly ground black pepper is one of my favorite flavors to combine with any fruity jam, jelly, or compote.

Since you're going to the trouble of making a dough from scratch, proofing it, rolling it out, cutting it, proofing it again, frying it, and dusting it—even before you realize that you need to figure out what the hell you're going to do with all that fryer oil once it cools—I understand that making the filling from scratch, too, might not be a top priority. I'll be completely honest: your favorite jelly or jam (as long as it's smooth enough to pipe) of any flavor will do the trick. However! I'd be remiss if I didn't campaign for you to give my Concord Grape and Manischewitz Jam a go. It combines my favorite fruit with my favorite wine made from my favorite fruit in one jar of purple perfection that was brought onto this planet to be squeezed into a fresh batch of *sufganiyot*.

RECIPE CONTINUES

FOR THE DOUGH

1 cup whole milk, heated to 115°F

¼ cup (50g) granulated sugar

1 (¼-ounce) packet active dry yeast (2¼ teaspoons)

4 ounces (1 stick) unsalted butter, melted

2 large eggs, at room temperature

4¼ cups (575g) all-purpose flour

1 teaspoon kosher salt

2 tablespoons vegetable oil

FOR FRYING AND FINISHING

Vegetable oil, for frying

½ cup (100g) granulated sugar

1 teaspoon kosher salt

1 teaspoon freshly ground black pepper

2 cups jam or jelly of your choice (preferably my Concord Grape and Manischewitz Jam, page 10)

1 For the dough: In the bowl of a stand mixer fitted with the whisk attachment, mix the warm milk and sugar to combine, then sprinkle the yeast over the top. Let stand until foamy, 5 to 10 minutes. Add the melted butter and eggs, then whisk on medium speed until incorporated.

2 Switch to the dough hook, then add the flour and salt to the bowl. Beginning on low speed and gradually increasing to medium, knead until a smooth, elastic dough forms, about 5 minutes.

3 Grease a medium bowl and your hands with the oil. Using your hands, transfer the dough to the bowl, gently turning it to coat it with oil, and shape it into a smooth ball. Cover with plastic wrap or a clean kitchen towel and set aside in a warm place until doubled in size, 1 hour to 1 hour 30 minutes.

4 Line a sheet pan with parchment paper. Transfer the dough to a lightly floured surface and roll it out to ½ inch thick. Using a 3-inch round cutter, cut out doughnuts and transfer them to the prepared pan. Gather the scraps, roll them out, and cut out more doughnuts so you have a total of 15 doughnuts; discard any remaining scraps of dough. Cover the rounds and set aside in a warm place again until puffy, about 45 minutes.

5 For frying and finishing the doughnuts: In a large Dutch oven, heat 2 inches of oil to 375°F. Line a half sheet pan with paper towels.

6 In a medium bowl, whisk together the sugar, salt, and pepper to combine. Place the jam or jelly in a piping bag fitted with a round piping tip.

7 Add five of the doughnuts to the hot oil and fry, flipping once, until golden brown and puffed, 1 to 2 minutes per side. Transfer to the paper towel–lined sheet pan to drain for 15 seconds. Before continuing with the next batch, toss each of the hot doughnuts in the sugar mixture to coat, then transfer them to a platter. Repeat to fry the remaining doughnuts in two more batches.

8 Using a paring knife, make a small cut at the top of each doughnut. Starting with the doughnuts you fried first, insert the tip of the piping bag into a doughnut and squeeze in 2 tablespoons of the jam or jelly. Repeat to fill the remaining doughnuts. Serve immediately while warm or within a few hours of frying for peak enjoyment.

Black-and-White Chocolate Chip Cookies

YIELD: MAKES ABOUT 24 COOKIES

PREP TIME: 30 MINUTES, PLUS 4 HOURS CHILLING TIME AND COOLING TIME

COOK TIME: 35 MINUTES

FOR THE COOKIES

8 ounces (2 sticks) unsalted butter, at room temperature

¾ cup packed (150g) light brown sugar

⅔ cup (135g) granulated sugar

2 large eggs

2 teaspoons vanilla extract

2 cups (270g) all-purpose flour

2 teaspoons kosher salt

¾ teaspoon baking soda

2 cups milk chocolate chips

3½ ounces dark chocolate (70 percent cacao), finely chopped

FOR THE WHITE CHOCOLATE GLAZE

1 cup white chocolate chips

3 tablespoons unrefined coconut oil

¾ cup confectioners' sugar

Pinch of kosher salt

FOR THE DARK CHOCOLATE GLAZE

1 cup dark chocolate chips

3 tablespoons unrefined coconut oil

¾ cup plus 2 tablespoons confectioners' sugar

Pinch of kosher salt

Flaky sea salt, for garnish (optional)

I'm just going to start by saying that black-and-white cookies are typically garbage. They will always be an iconic Jewish sweet that we should celebrate and respect, but I'm not going to pretend that most bakeries haven't been missing the mark in their execution, leaving the cookies either too dry, too eggy, too sweet, or just too one-note. That's when I decided to do the unthinkable: flip a chocolate chip cookie upside down and cover it with a combo of white and dark chocolate glazes. In the words of Lady Gaga, "Brilliant, incredible, amazing, showstopping, spectacular, never the same, totally unique, completely not ever been done before."

My love of chocolate chip cookies knows no bounds, and I always have a batch of dough scooped and frozen for a last-minute sweet for entertaining or a late-night case of the munchies. Given its combo of vanilla-scented dough packed with chocolate chunks, it's kind of a poetically perfect vessel for the two flavors of glaze living side by side on top. Using just a few more chocolate chips, some confectioners' sugar, and coconut oil, these glazes fall somewhere between ganache and Magic Shell, and set with a matte finish for easy decorating.

While the secret to eating them is still to get a little of both sides in each bite, there's no world in which you'll be able to have just one. Eat your heart out, Seinfeld—this is the only cookie I'll be looking to now!

1 For the cookies: In the bowl of a stand mixer fitted with the paddle attachment, cream the butter and both sugars on medium speed until light and fluffy, 2 minutes. With the mixer running, add the eggs one at a time and mix until incorporated, stopping to scrape the sides of the bowl as needed. Add the vanilla and mix to incorporate.

2 Add the flour, kosher salt, and baking soda and mix on low speed until a smooth dough forms. Add the milk chocolate chips and dark chocolate and mix on low speed until just incorporated. Remove the mixer bowl, cover, and refrigerate the dough for at least 4 hours or preferably overnight.

RECIPE CONTINUES

3 Preheat the oven to 350°F. Line two half sheet pans with parchment paper and have a 5-inch-wide bowl or round cutter ready.

4 Scoop the cookie dough into ¼-cup balls. Working in two batches, place 6 cookies on each of the prepared pans, spacing them 3 inches apart. Bake for 14 to 16 minutes, until golden brown. As soon as you remove each pan from the oven, place the bowl or round cutter over each cookie and gently roll it around in gentle circles to smooth the edges into a perfect round. Let the cookies cool slightly on the pans, then transfer to a wire rack to cool completely. Repeat with the remaining balls of cookie dough. Once all the cookies are baked and cooled, divide them between the two sheet pans, with the bottom (flat side) of each cookie facing up.

5 For the white chocolate glaze: Set a medium metal bowl over a small pot of simmering water. Put the white chocolate chips and coconut oil in the bowl and heat, stirring as needed, until melted and well combined. Remove the bowl from the heat and whisk in the confectioners' sugar and kosher salt until smooth and glossy. Using an offset spatula or butter knife, spread the glaze over half of the bottom (flat side) of each cookie to coat.

6 For the dark chocolate glaze: Set another medium metal bowl over the pot of simmering water. Put the dark chocolate chips and coconut oil in the bowl and heat, stirring as needed, until melted and well combined. Remove the bowl from the heat and whisk in the confectioners' sugar and kosher salt until smooth and glossy. Using an offset spatula or butter knife, spread the glaze over the other half of the bottom of each cookie to coat.

7 Garnish with flaky sea salt, if desired. Refrigerate for 15 minutes to set the glaze, then serve.

Salted Chocolate-Cardamom Cookies

YIELD: MAKES 24 COOKIES

PREP TIME: 20 MINUTES, PLUS 45 MINUTES CHILLING TIME

COOK TIME: 25 MINUTES

1 pound dark chocolate (70 percent cacao), chopped (2⅔ cups)

⅓ cup extra-virgin olive oil

¾ cup (102g) all-purpose flour

1½ teaspoons kosher salt

1 teaspoon baking powder

1 teaspoon ground cardamom

4 large eggs

1 cup (200g) granulated sugar

½ cup packed (100g) light brown sugar

Flaky sea salt, for garnish

So, this recipe was born of rock-bottom desperation. I threw it together last minute before break-fast for Yom Kippur, because the Bundt cake I had originally made stuck to pan and tore in half, along with my heart. When you remember that I was fasting during this whole ordeal, you can imagine how dramatic I was being. Fighting back tears, I scavenged through my pantry, trying to piece something together even though I was low on flour, time, and patience. Of course, I made it work, and by the time I was stuffing my face with whitefish salad, all that heartbreak was but a distant memory!

These beautifully crinkled and cracked dark chocolate cookies are perfumed with cardamom and garnished with flaky sea salt for the perfect sweet-and-salty treat with a most magical warmth that lingers with every bite. The trick to making them is in the temperature of the dough. Primarily made of ganache, the dough needs to be chilled slightly to set, or it will be too runny to scoop. The sweet spot for the perfect firmness is 45 minutes in the fridge; leave it in too long, and your dough will be hard as a rock, which won't be fun to scoop! Immediately after you bake them, make sure to follow my trick for flawlessly round cookies: take a small bowl or round cutter, just larger than the cookie, and roll it in gentle circles around the edges to smooth the cookie into a perfect round—not mandatory, but a surefire way to never serve another oblong cookie again.

1 Preheat the oven to 350°F. Line two half sheet pans with parchment paper.

2 Set a medium metal bowl over a small pot of simmering water. Put the chocolate and olive oil in the bowl and heat, stirring as needed, until melted and well combined. Remove the bowl from the heat.

3 Meanwhile, in a medium bowl, whisk together the flour, kosher salt, baking powder, and cardamom.

4 In a large bowl, whisk together the eggs, granulated sugar, and brown sugar until thick and lightened in color, about 2 minutes. Slowly whisk in the melted chocolate mixture, then gently fold in the dry ingredients until a smooth dough forms. Cover and refrigerate for 45 minutes.

5 Scoop the dough into 2-tablespoon balls, rolling each gently with your hands to smooth it, and place on the prepared sheet pans, spacing the cookies 2 inches apart. You should have 12 cookies per pan. Sprinkle a pinch of flaky sea salt over each ball of dough. Bake, rotating the pans halfway through, for 10 to 12 minutes, until the cookies are puffed and just starting to crack on the surface.

6 Let cool completely on the pans, then serve.

drinks

Sumac Hot Chocolate

YIELD: MAKES ABOUT 4 CUPS

PREP TIME: 5 MINUTES

COOK TIME: 5 MINUTES

3 cups whole milk

¼ cup honey

2 teaspoons ground sumac

½ teaspoon kosher salt

6 ounces dark chocolate (70 percent cacao), chopped (1 cup)

Whipped cream, for serving

If you take anything away from this entire cookbook, I want it to be that you should always have sumac in your pantry, and you should be pairing it with chocolate. It adds the perfect punch of acidity to make even shitty-quality chocolate taste fancy. So you can only imagine the flavor you get when you pair it with those top-shelf bars! This hot chocolate was born out of cozy weekends spent up in the Hudson Valley with friends and family in the fall. I pack the trunk of our car with all the provisions to cook up a storm, including half of my spice cabinet. Naturally, some sumac made its way into a pot of hot chocolate to sip by the fire.

While this recipe was ideated in the colder months, you can also chill it to make chocolate milk that puts any school cafeteria to shame. Great for kids! Great for adults who eat/act like kids!

In a medium saucepan, combine the milk, honey, sumac, and salt. Bring to a simmer over medium-high heat, then remove from the heat and whisk in the chocolate until smooth. Divide among glasses, top with whipped cream, and serve.

Make It an Egg Cream!
(pictured on page 234)
A New York classic that doesn't actually contain eggs, or cream! One of my father's favorite drinks, a chocolate egg cream is essentially chocolate milk—that must be made with Fox's U-Bet syrup, according to him—and seltzer mixed into a creamy, bubbly beverage that gives any fountain drink a run for its money. Chill this hot chocolate and pour it over ice to fill a glass halfway, then top with cold seltzer and serve with a straw.

Fresh Mint Tea

YIELD: SERVES 1

TOTAL TIME: 5 MINUTES

1 tablespoon honey

4 sprigs mint

1 slice lemon

Boiling water

Fresh mint tea is the Middle Eastern equivalent of old Ashkenazi women ordering hot water with lemon at every restaurant. Given that it's caffeine-free, it's become my favorite way to end the day or just a dinner of overeating. The best part is how simple it is. It's a calming elixir that I'm always stocked to brew at a moment's notice.

In a mug, combine the honey, mint, and lemon, pressing them into the mug to fit. Cover with boiling water and let steep for 3 to 4 minutes, then enjoy.

Manischewitz Rum Punch

YIELD: MAKES ABOUT 3 QUARTS,
TO SERVE 12

PREP TIME: 10 MINUTES

1 (750ml) bottle Manischewitz wine

1 (750ml) bottle white rum

1 (750ml) bottle white grape juice

2 cups seltzer water

¾ cup canned pineapple juice

½ cup freshly squeezed orange juice

½ cup freshly squeezed lemon juice

1 tablespoon Angostura bitters

Ice (see headnote), for serving

This punch tastes like college, but in a good way. While Manischewitz may be polarizing as a wine, as a mixer, it's kind of perfect. The sugary notes of the Concord grape wine blend with white rum and a rainbow of fruit juices for a take on the tropical cocktail that'll truly raise your spirits. And by spirits, I mean BAC.

If you're looking to get fancy, it's time to crack out the Bundt pan to make a chic ice block for your punch bowl. Line the pan with grapes and citrus slices, then cover with water and freeze. To remove, simply dip the bottom of the pan into a bowl of warm water and then pop your ice Bundt straight into this rum punch.

In a large punch bowl, stir together the Manischewitz, rum, grape juice, seltzer, pineapple juice, orange juice, lemon juice, and bitters with ice until well chilled, then serve.

Soda and Bitters Bar

Seltzer: Tall glass, zero sodium, over ice.

~8 dashes bitters: I always have Angostura and Peychaud's bitters on hand, which add anise notes, but the bitters options are endless, so find one that you love.

Garnish: I try to have rosemary sprigs, thyme sprigs, lemon wheels, lime wheels, and grapefruit twists for mixing and matching.

Optional libations: Vodka, gin, maybe even arak. Pretty much anything clear. 1 ounce to spike, 2 ounces to turn up.

Okay, so I'm not much of a drinker. My weak Jewish stomach has led me to live a Cali sober life, which is why you only get one cocktail recipe in this book. For me, it's all about the soda and bitters, combining Jewish champagne (seltzer) with a few dashes of the botanical digestif to quench my thirst and keep my stomach happy. But at the same time, I have a full bar that all my guests are free to raid whenever they come over. This has led me to have a carefully curated mix of ingredients on hand so anyone can make their glass of ephemeral effervescence, as well as spike it, if they want to give those hard seltzer companies a run for their money. This isn't a recipe, per se, but some guidelines to make you seem like a relaxed host/bartender.

acknowledgments

First and foremost, thank you to my husband, Alex. You're my best taste-tester, my best proof-reader, and my best friend. Thank you to my mother for being the source of so much material for this book and such an enthusiastic cheerleader of everything I do. Thank you to my father for always being a beacon of support throughout my entire career in food. Thank you, Jamie, for being the best sister I could ever ask for. I'm so thankful you brought Manu into our family, and that he eats everything that you won't. Thank you to my grandma Annie for showing me at a young age the power of cooking for those you love. Thank you to my aunt Susi for being a source of knowledge on our family's recipes and teaching me how to properly cook a brisket. Thank you to my late grandma Marilyn, who introduced me to the magic of the New York restaurant scene and was so excited for this book.

I'm so incredibly thankful to all of Alex's family for opening my eyes to a whole new world of Jewish food. Thank you to my mother-in-law, Robina Shapiro, for welcoming me with open arms into your family and kitchen, helping me learn and preserve many of these recipes. Thank you to Alex's aunt Diana Phillips for being a constant source of hospitality and culinary inspiration. Thank you to my brother-in-law Avi Savar and sister-in-law Leigh Savar for not only your friendship and mentorship, but for the blessing of blending my family with Leigh's to give us an ever-growing seder table. Thank you to Kristen Stillwell for taking my author photo in quarantine and giving life to my campy challah picture day idea!

Given that this is my first book, there were so many people helping me along this journey. Thank you to my agent, Stacey Glick, for being such a wonderful guide on this maiden voyage. Thank you to Kate Heddings and Justin Chapple for introducing me to Stacey. Thank you to Erin McDowell and Olia Hercules for sharing your book proposals and words of encouragement with me. Thank you to my first editor Justin Schwartz for working with me through the photo shoot and to my second editor Sarah Pelz for taking over seamlessly and helping truly execute my vision. Special thanks to Sarah Passick for pointing me in the right direction throughout the whole process! Lucky to have you, Allison Milam, and Dan Geneen in my life.

Thank you to Gillian Feinglass for being the most incredible recipe tester in the world. Your talent is only topped by your work ethic and kindness. Thank you to all my other recipe testers who helped make this book perfect: Jessica Cohen, Sam Goldberg, Dr. Pam, Dana Golub, Emily Rubano, Ranleigh Zoe, Alex Dashefsky, Alexandra Weiner, and Nick Ruhrkraut.

None of this would have been possible with the best team to shoot this book in the beginning of a pandemic! Thank you to Matt Taylor

Gross for putting your heart and talent into every photo. Thank you to Barrett Washburne for making every dish way prettier than I could ever have. Thank you to Marie Sullivan for taking my vision and so expertly curating the props to reflect it. Thank you to all of the kitchen assistants: Andrea Loret de Mola, Cass Rafsol, Lauren Radel, Spencer Richards, and Mark Vasquez.

Thank you to Julie and Dan Resnick for being so supportive of this entire process and giving me free range to use the Feedfeed studio for everything from wild Shabbats to the book shoot.

Thank you to OneTable for bringing the ritual of Shabbat into my life, which helped me truly discover the pride I have in being Jewish. Thank you to every guest who's ever sat at my table and allowed me to test my recipes in action. A special thanks to Evan Ross Katz, Billy Jacobson, Austin Friedman, and Michael Maniawski for becoming the close friend group Alex and I dreamed of making when we started hosting Shabbat.

And, of course, thank you to the Jews. I love being Jewish!

index

Note: Page references in *italics* indicate photographs.

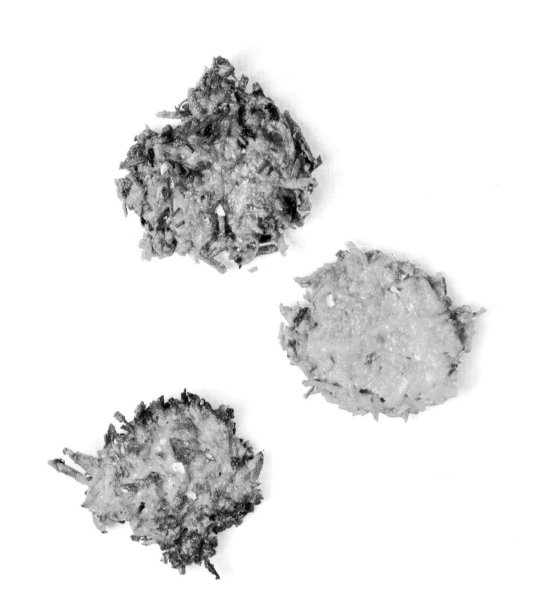